Deny & Disavow

Distancing the Imperial Past in the Culture Wars

Alan Lester

SunRise

SunRise

First published in Great Britain in 2022 by SunRise

Second Edition (Revised) published in 2023

SunRise Publishing Ltd
124 City Road
London EC1V 2NX

ISBN 978-1-9144891-4-3

Copyright © Alan Lester

The right of Alan Lester to be identified as the author of this work has been asserted by him in accordance with the Copyright, Designs and Patents Act 1988.

All rights reserved. No part of this publication may be reproduced, stored in or introduced into a retrieval system, or transmitted, in any form, or by any means (electronic, mechanical, photocopying, recording or otherwise) without the prior written permission of the publisher. Any person who performs an unauthorised act in relation to this publication may be liable to criminal prosecution and civil claims for damages.

A CIP catalogue record for this book is available from the British Library.

Typeset in Minion Pro and Impact.

Deny & Disavow is essential reading for academics, journalists, students, legislators and all those who want to better understand today's key polemics.

Leading academics, journalists and opinion formers have welcomed this unique book which has been extensively revised and updated since first publication in 2022.

'*Deny & Disavow is an essential guide. Written by a man with three decades of experience of researching imperial history, and combining elements of memoir with travelogue, it is incredibly accessible, totally authoritative, and intensely readable. This country would be infinitely more sane if it were compulsory reading.*'

Sathnam Sanghera, award-winning author, columnist and feature writer for *The Times*.

'This concise, but invaluable, book provides insights into nineteenth-century views of empire which now animate twenty-first century culture wars, from Edward Colston's toppled statue to the Common Sense Group of Conservative MPs and Peers. Professor Lester's book provides a powerful antidote to historical denial and omission as well as a plea for more rational, evidence-based views of the past.'

Corrine Fowler, author and Professor of Postcolonial Literature at the University of Leicester.

"It is incumbent on those of us who are interested in serious discussion of the British Empire and its legacies to be prepared to respond reasonably and convincingly when we are challenged. This book could be just the thing."

Ryan Hanley, Imperial and Global Forum blog.

'A hugely informative and highly readable takedown of the self-serving canards spread by Britain's culture warriors on the question of empire. Lester takes us on a figurative stroll through Britain's imperial history, past statues and stately homes, explaining why a challenging historical engagement is better than either shame or myths of glory.'

Priyamvada Gopal, author of *Insurgent Empire: Anticolonial Resistance and British Dissent*, and Professor of Postcolonial Studies in the Faculty of English at the University of Cambridge.

'Alan Lester's Deny & Disavow *is a timely guidebook to the culture wars surrounding Britain's contested past. With wit and gentle exasperation, Lester shows how to counter the arguments of imperial nostalgism, and insist on the real complexity of history: a complexity that is always ethically challenging, always difficult, and always resistant to the comforts of triumphalism.'*

Peter Mitchell, Author of *Imperial Nostalgia: How the British Conquered Themselves*

Contents

Acknowledgements	9
Preface	11
PART ONE	18
Britain's Imperial History Through Statues	18
Introduction: Colston and the Culture War	19
What is Culture War?	26
CHAPTER ONE: Walking Westminster: Seacole and Clive	33
Clive and India	38
CHAPTER TWO: Wolseley	44
Sir Garnet Wolseley and the Expansion of Empire	44
Opium Wars	55
Confederation Wars	60
CHAPTER THREE: Bartle Frere and Rhodes	64
Cecil Rhodes and southern Africa	70
PART TWO	81
Empire in the Culture War	82
CHAPTER FOUR: The Culture War in Parliament	82
Common Sense	82
The Red Wall	83
Emotional Attachments	86
Race	91
CHAPTER FIVE: The Race Report	96
Understanding History	97
Creating Britishness	99
Decolonising	100
CHAPTER SIX: Heritage	106
Restore Trust	106
Our Newspapers	113

CHAPTER SEVEN: Academia	116
History Reclaimed	118
PART THREE	**130**
Glaring Omissions	131
CHAPTER EIGHT: A Year in the life of the British Empire	131
1838: A Year in the Empire	132
January–April	135
May–August	141
September–December	144
CHAPTER NINE: India and the Settler Colonies	147
The Raj	**147**
The Settler and Crown Colonies	152
Well-meant Genocide	156
CHAPTER TEN: British Humanitarians: the 'Good' Imperialists	162
Backlash: The Invention of the Proto-Woke	168
CHAPTER ELEVEN: There's No Moral Balance Sheet for the British Empire	174
Late Imperialism	181
The Empire Comes Home, or We are Here Because You Were There	185
CHAPTER TWELVE: What Are the British Empire's 'Legacies'?	191
Continuities/Discontinuities	191
Built and Institutional Legacies	195
Nostalgia	198
Agency	199
Conclusion: Seven Apologists' Arguments	**202**
Selected Further Reading	**210**
References	**214**
Index	**238**

This book is dedicated to the inspirational Karen Munn

ACKNOWLEDGEMENTS

Thank you to my wonderful dad and brother for the love and support that's kept me going since the loss of my mum in 2019, my diagnosis with Primary Sclerosing Cholangitis the following year, my liver transplant and my subsequent surgery and ongoing treatment for cancer of the bile duct.

I would not have got to this point without the PSC specialists and Gastro team at St Thomas' Hospital and the hard-working staff of the Alan Apley ward. My sincerest gratitude for the work you do, your patience as I bombarded you with questions, and your kindness. Thanks especially to Dr Sreelakshmi Kotha and Dr Phillip Berry. My deepest gratitude to the Liver specialists at King's College Hospital, and especially to Ms Miriam Cortes for the skill and compassion with which she carried out both my transplant and subsequent Whipple Procedure, and to the chemotherapy and radiotherapy teams at Guy's, including Drs Sarker and Doss.

I am grateful to Gurdeep Mattu of SunRise Publishing for the initial approach to write this book. It's taken me in a new direction at just the right time. The untiring anti-racist activist Jacqui Stanford and Adam Smethurst also pushed me in that direction. Thank you. I am very grateful to the mums' and dads' club of Uckfield for friendship and support, and for helping me think how best to put things. Not all of them agree with me, but life would be boring if they did. In alphabetical order of mum first, so as not to indicate preference that might come back to bite me: Debbie and Nige, Jen and Ian, Jessica and Alex, Jo and Nick, the late and much missed Karen, and David, Kim and Mog, Mel and Darren, Net and Pat, Verity and Rich, and Zoe and Lee.

Ian McGukin has been a great cycling friend, encouraging me to keep riding as and when I can and lending me some beautiful coffee table books about bikes when I haven't been up to reading much else. The 'bike blokes book club' have been a great source of support.

Ian and Chloe, Matt and Fee and Ewan and Sarah have been there to help me out morally and practically and I'll always be grateful.

At work, I am forever in debt to Mike Collyer, Fae Dussart, Buzz Harrison, Dave Ockwell and Simon Rycroft, for covering for me, utterly selflessly. Thanks to Fae also for reading a draft and helping me to put some things right. It has been a real pleasure, as well as a marvellous learning opportunity, to work with Nicola Thomas and the Exeter team on the reinterpretation of the Sir Redvers Buller statue. Over the years Catherine Hall has exemplified for me what it is to be a scholar of empire and Britain. It helps to have a role model like her.

Above all, thank you for putting up with me Jo, Daisy, Evan, Alfred (and Nellie our rescue dog, who has kept me exercising and my spirits up). You're what makes everything worthwhile.

PREFACE

Over the last few years we have seen people in the Conservative government under Boris Johnson then, briefly, Liz Truss and at the time of writing, Rishi Sunak, energise an unprecedented and disturbing 'culture war'. Culture war is a phenomenon first defined by James Davison Hunter in the USA, in which 'Politics becomes a proxy for cultural positions that simply won't brook any kind of dissent or argument'. It is a form of tribalism that began in the 1960s, with conservative institutions resisting the advances in civil rights for women and African Americans. It reached new levels of intensity with Donald Trump's populist backlash after Barack Obama's Presidency. Here in the UK, a buoyant, post-Brexit, populist wing of the Conservative Party, with relentlessly vociferous supporters in the press and a handful of supporters in academia, are waging their own rhetorical war on those who propose antiracist, environmental and gender related reforms, using the word 'woke' as a sneering, catch-all descriptor for such people. Young people who are sensitive to these issues are dismissed as 'snowflakes' and accused of adopting a 'cancel culture' by daring to speak out. The expertise of those who research uncomfortable facts has been dismissed by the most prominent of politicians.

Deny & Disavow

A key part of these conservative political activities has been an attack on those who would undermine a long-cherished view of the British Empire. This book, based on thirty years of collaborative research, writing, and scholarship on that Empire, is written in response.

For a scholar of British colonialism, witnessing the explosion of polarised and simplistic argumentation over the Empire's legacies in the last few years feels like a glimpse of what virologists and vaccinologists must have experienced as public discussion of Covid-19 exploded. As with so much of our post-Brexit politics, complexity, honesty and integrity in public discussions of Empire have become rare commodities.

Most professional historians of British colonialism, of whom I know many, base their research on evidence while admitting its limitations. They strive for objectivity whilst recognising that it is evasive, and they are driven by curiosity rather than contemporary politics, seeking to mitigate the ways in which the latter inevitably shapes the former. They are far from being the Marxist/Critical Race Theory — inspired radicals portrayed by some journalists and politicians. Their implicit distaste for unprovoked invasion and racism stems from their humanity and basic morality. It is not directed solely and vindictively against 'the British' and it is not the result of a 'Far Left' political disposition. For the most part they refuse to be drawn into the culture war's polarising binaries. In the meantime, however, a wider section of society is being exposed to politicised caricatures of the British Empire that do an active disservice to the public understanding of history.

For decades, even centuries, British apologists for the Empire have claimed it was, overall, a force for good: an engine of globalisation, free trade, the beneficial spread of

Preface

the English language, economically vital infrastructure and new ideas of governance. These ideas have been articulated since the middle of the nineteenth century, when the British Empire emerged from a period of transition after the Napoleonic War, grew and consolidated, and when the technological changes of steam and telegraph, pioneered in Europe and the USA, were harnessed worldwide. Britons have been assured ever since, in popular books, the press and on TV, that their empire was beneficial not just for them and their numerous 'native' collaborators, but generally, for the people they colonised and their descendants. This is the powerful national myth that I believed growing up, and that today's culture warriors are determined to cling to. Like all such national mythologies, it has germs of truth, but it is rooted in the propaganda of the imperial period itself.

Both historians' enquiries into how the British Empire operated and Black Lives Matter activists' focus on its enduring racial inequalities, render this myth no longer tenable in contemporary Britain. It is a story that not only tells nothing like the whole truth of the Empire, but which serves actively to divide White from Black Britons. It stands in the way of a better Britain.

The overwhelming majority of historical experts on colonialism, working on an enormous documentary record spread across The National Archives, the British Library, national and local state libraries and hundreds of private collections around the world, now testify that: British colonisation involved great violence against people of colour around the world; that colonised people of colour were generally subordinated to White colonists (for example they had to show deference to White people in everyday encounters, they incurred more severe judicial penalties for the same offences, and they suffered from restricted voting rights); that most White Britons considered it common sense that they were superior to people of colour (not necessarily biologically but culturally) — an attitude that we call racism today; that as Empire retreated and Britons of colour came to the UK in greater numbers, they met a widespread view that Black citizens did not belong here; and that certain British politicians have amplified and stoked this view of racially exclusive belonging beyond the end of Empire.

There is, then, a far more obvious characteristic of the British Empire than its selective spreading of economic and political opportunity. It is striking to anyone who has done any serious research on it. The British Empire was a vehicle for establishing, maintaining and justifying White supremacy on a global scale, and for persuading generations of Britons that ours is a White island that keeps colonised subjects of colour in their place overseas. It was not the only such vehicle, since the other European empires of the seventeenth to the twentieth centuries had similar effects, but Britain's was the largest, the most influential across multiple continents, and has of course shaped Britain itself most powerfully. The British Empire's global presence is the main reason why today's Britain is so multi-cultural and we need to take the divergent experiences of Empire associated with our diverse communities into account in our national history.

As I will show in this book, the benefits that propagandists for this Empire point to — free trade, linguistic convergence, railways, schools, and participatory governance — operated overwhelmingly on behalf of White Britons for most of the empire's existence, even if they also benefited some among subordinate elites. The British beneficiaries of Empire included many of those who stayed at home as well as their kin who emigrated to become colonists and settlers with

Preface

Black servants, free or cheap land and exalted social status. The costs of colonialism were racked up largely, although never exclusively, against British subjects of colour who were consistently denied the rights of White Britons. We now know far more about the role of slave trading and slave ownership in enriching British society. But long after Britain abolished slavery — an act often proclaimed in imperial propaganda as the end of British colonialism's 'bad phase' — White Britons conquered viable, independent societies comprised of people who had darker skins than themselves. They did so with great violence, facilitated by overwhelming firepower. Sometimes they justified their invasions and usurpations as measures taken to combat slavery and other forms of oppression in indigenous societies (which undoubtedly existed), but more often they simply took it for granted that people of colour would be better off governed by White people, because the latter were superior. Even Winston Churchill, the darling of populist defenders of empire, admitted that 'our claim to be left in the unmolested enjoyment of vast and splendid possessions, mainly acquired by violence, largely maintained by force, often seems less reasonable to others than to us'.[1]

British colonists coerced conquered people of colour into working for them all over the world and assumed ownership of their resources throughout the eighteenth, nineteenth and early twentieth centuries. Where they signed treaties with indigenous allies to fight against rival European colonists, promising to limit their own presence and impact, most notably in North America, they generally went on to break them.

Relations between Britons and indigenous peoples varied enormously across a quarter of the Earth's land surface (at the early twentieth century empire's greatest extent) and over 300 years. The indulged princes and merchants of post-Uprising India experienced empire very differently from the Aboriginal people of southern Australia, who resisted annihilation in the early nineteenth century. But everywhere, colonial administration rested on an everyday distinction — a 'rule of difference' as the Indian historian Partha Chatterjee has put it — between the different races. Black lives tended not to matter as much as White lives.

Yet historians who draw attention to the racial thinking and discriminatory practice that fundamentally underpinned the Empire are now condemned by populist, right wing culture warriors. In the wake of the Black Lives Matter challenge, a relatively few, but very well publicised commentators have managed to twist the practising of history as 'censoring', 'trashing' or even 'destroying' our national past. Historians, along with antiracist activists, have found themselves accused of being part of an imaginary 'woke' conspiracy against all that Britain stands for.

The backlash has come overwhelmingly from those whose self-esteem is closely tied to a group identity defined by long-established ideas of Britishness. The strategies for deflecting from historical facts which threaten that identity include denying the accuracy of the information provided by historians; blaming the victims of colonial acts of violence, claiming that colonial rule was necessary or enacted with good intentions; focusing on the sacrifices made by colonists, and above all, 'whataboutery': pointing out the bad things that other groups have also done in the past, or are doing now.[2]

I did not write this book to 'trash Britain'. I do not consider myself 'woke' and I am not a Marxist radical. Since the first edition of this book came out, like other serious historians, I have been accused by some of the figures mentioned here of

Preface

being part of a CRT (Critical Race Theory) 'religion', inspired by analyses of the White privilege entrenched in American institutions. In fact, my work on the British Empire has been based on its own archives and upon concepts that scholars of colonialism have discussed and refined over many decades. I have affection rather than loathing for many of the Britons who lived and died in the Empire, having become familiar with them through biographical research over the years. I do not think contemporary Britons bear personal responsibility for the actions of their predecessors, nor that they should feel ashamed. I do not think that Britons were exceptionally good or evil and I think that trying to say whether the British Empire was 'better' or 'worse' than other empires, before, after or contemporaneous with Britain's, is reductive and irrelevant for our debates on its legacies in Britain.

I do think, though, that when we revisit British history with the acknowledgement that Black lives matter too, it changes the dominant national story that I and my peers were brought up to believe in. It reveals just how selective and discriminatory is the version of British history defended by some of today's social conservatives. If we are to begin to address the structural inequalities of race, inherited from centuries of colonialism in this country, we need to wean ourselves off seeing the essence of Britishness in a White supremacist empire.

Part One

Britain's Imperial History Through Statues

Introduction

Colston and the Culture War

Bristol, June 2020

In June 2020, after the police murder of George Floyd in the USA, and amid the global COVID-19 pandemic, Black Lives Matter activists invited Britons to reflect on the pernicious role of racism in our society. Far from being a distraction from the pandemic, their protest was fuelled by it. The mortality rate from COVID for Black men was running at 256 per 100,000, while for White men it was 87 per 100,000, and Black women were dying at the rate of 120 per 100,000, with White women at 52 per 100,000.[3] Much of the variation was due to the over-representation of Black people in public-facing service roles along with housing and health inequalities which themselves reflected stubborn racial inequality.[4] Protestors in Bristol focused their activity on the statue of the late seventeenth century slave trader Edward Colston. Colston had directly donated to schools and churches as well as founding a boys' school and almshouse. Colston Girls' School was established from his endowments.[5]

Statues, however, are products of the time that they were put up rather than of the time of their subjects' lives. Colston's was erected over 170 years after he had died, in 1895. It was only in the mid-1890s that middle class Bristolians believed that an act of civic unity and pride, focused on a

Deny & Disavow

'Cult of Colston', might serve contemporary purposes. In 1889–90 there had been a wave of strikes in Bristol as well as campaigns for municipal intervention in dire working-class living conditions. The philanthropy of the local aristocracy was not enough to hold such agitation at bay and so the city's Society of Merchant Venturers decided to venerate the long-dead figure of Colston to rally the middle classes to greater charitable efforts. Putting up his statue was an attempt to head

Black Lives Matter protesters push the statue of Edward Colston into Bristol Harbour. Photograph: NurPhoto/Getty Images

Introduction: Colston and the Culture War

off further instability by persuading Bristol's working classes that middle class benevolence, modelled on that of Colston's nearly two centuries before, would attend to their needs.[6]

Colston had acquired much of the wealth that he dispensed in Bristol as a member of the Royal African Company. Its business model was based on the monopoly, granted by King Charles II, of a well-established English trade in enslaved people. Colston was both a shareholder and the company's deputy governor in 1689-90. During the period in which he was most active, the Company purchased over 84,000 African adult and child captives and transported them across the Atlantic, packed as commodities in ships' holds. They were a fraction of the 3.25 million African captives trafficked by British slave traders in some 12,000 voyages, to ensure that Europe's sweet tooth could be satisfied with lucrative sugar imports from Caribbean plantations.

In 1682, John Babot described how African intermediaries brought captives to the coast from distant homes inland, in collar chains and ankle fetters. On the beach, European surgeons inspected them and selected those young and healthy enough for purchase. Each of those 'passed as good, is marked on the breast with a red hot iron, imprinting the mark of the French, English or Dutch companies, that so each nation may distinguish their own, and to prevent their being chang'd by the natives for worse, as they are apt to do. In this particular, care is taken that the women, as tenderest, be not burnt too hard'.[7]

Colston's company branded its human 'property' with its own RAC logo before embarking them on the 1–2 month 'middle passage' across the Atlantic. For most of the voyage, captives were kept below decks in chains to prevent the kind of insurrection that was known to take place on around 10 per cent of the passages. A century later, when conditions on the slave ships had marginally improved, a former ship's captain turned antislavery campaigner, John Newton, described the conditions in the slave holds as 'almost insupportable to a person not accustomed to them ... They are kept down, often by the weather, to breathe a hot and corrupted air ... this, added to the galling of their irons, and the despondency which seizes their spirits [and the facility with which disease spread when shared buckets of urine and faeces were overflowing] ... soon becomes fatal'. [8]

Some 19,000 of the Royal African Company's captives died on the journey whilst Colston was in charge. Once in the Caribbean colonies, the Company sold the survivors to new, predominantly White 'owners', so that they could be worked in the cultivation mainly of sugar and tobacco in hot, humid conditions. If they resisted or attempted to escape, overseers would punish them with flogging, mutilation or death. Enslaved women were routinely raped by their owners. The motive was not only sexual violence but also economic. Enslaved women's children became the slave owners' property, to be sold on to other planters or retained as their owners wished.

For years, activists in Bristol, a city whose wealth was especially dependent on this dehumanising business for 180 years, had been trying to get the local authorities to do something about both the statue and the other memorials to Colston littering the city. It takes but a modicum of empathy to understand the offence that the plaque on the statue's plinth, describing this slave trader as 'one of the most virtuous and wise sons of their city', might cause descendants of enslaved West Indians. But the majority of Bristol's residents, mostly ignorant of Colston's activities, had no concerns about it.

An attempt to get a second plaque added, which explained

Introduction: Colston and the Culture War

Colston's role in the slave trade, had stalled, largely due to the obstruction of a Conservative local councillor, who objected to any wording that adequately conveyed the scale of the RAC's atrocities. Indeed, somewhat ironically in hindsight, he thought vandalising or stealing any such plaque 'may be justified'. The attempt to add historical context to the statue was seen as detracting from 'history'. What mattered was the version of history with which most Bristolians were comfortable rather than any historical reality.

The *Bristol Post* described what happened in June 2020 as reaction to the murder of George Floyd in the USA spread among Black communities and their allies in Britain: 'And so, with no ongoing public discussion about the statue, petitions created, signed and submitted over the years, and a second plaque project failing to become reality, 10,000 protesters filed past the statue of Edward Colston on Sunday afternoon [of 7th June]. The city council had covered it with a dark tarpaulin. It took approximately four minutes from the time that the first protester scaled the plinth to the moment the statue crashed to the ground.'[9] In pulling down the statue and dumping it in the harbour, the protestors made it clear that a reckoning with the history of the British Empire was long overdue.

One would expect the authorities to condemn the unsanctioned toppling of the statue, as did Bristol's Black mayor, Marvin Rees. It was, after all, a matter of civic vandalism subsequently condoned by the jury that acquitted the 'Colston Four'. But whereas Rees then accepted the opportunity to engage with the hundreds of thousands across the country who sympathised with the protestors' cause, and sought to find a way forward through dialogue, the central government's strategy was immediately one of distancing, denial and disavowal. Its ongoing response has been to mobilise a backlash to Black Lives Matter through culture war.

In the immediate aftermath of Colston's toppling, Housing, Communities and Local Government Secretary Robert Jenrick declared 'We will save Britain's statues from the woke militants who want to censor our past'.[10] Then Digital, Culture and Media Secretary Oliver Dowden instructed Britain's leading museums, galleries and heritage organisations that they 'must defend our culture and history from the noisy minority of activists constantly trying to do Britain down'.[11] Dowden's successor, Nadine Dorries, was even more hard line, the *Daily Mail* saying that she was promoted specifically 'to fight the woke warriors at culture'.[12]

These ministers' rhetoric was inspired and then reinforced by allies in the press. There is now a relentless barrage of articles and editorials, day after day, in the *Mail, Express, Telegraph* and *Spectator,* and on GB News too, waging a 'war on woke'. These media outlets conjure up images of hordes of militants tearing around the country pulling down statues, taking down portraits of the Queen, dishonouring the Union Jack, indoctrinating schoolchildren and visitors to stately homes, museums and botanic gardens, and ruining the last night of the Proms. They condemned the England football team for the 'toxic' act of taking the knee in the Euro 2020/21 finals, desisting only when the team became a popular symbol of modern, interracial, Britain despite their best efforts. They rail against academics and heritage organisations seeking to provide greater knowledge of Britain's still largely suppressed imperial history, and they fuel extremist White nationalist hate — now the largest security threat in many parts of the country.

So where did this culture war backlash come from and why is it being waged? After all, most Black Lives Matter

Introduction: Colston and the Culture War

protesters simply called for a recognition of Black Britons' ancestors' suffering as part of our shared national story, and, more importantly, meaningful attempts to redress ongoing racism and racial inequalities.[13] There are, I think, two main reasons why the more extreme populist conservatives are so determined to centre their attempted culture war on the movement. One is about short-term politicking and the other, much more deeply held emotional attachments. I will investigate these in greater depth.

What is Culture War?

First though, we need to see where the notion of culture war as political strategy has come from. Primarily, although not exclusively, it has been an American phenomenon. James Davison Hunter first applied the term 'culture war' in 1991.[14] He was referring to the attempt by otherwise disparate groups including Christian fundamentalists, Orthodox Jews, and conservative Catholics, to resist a tendency towards secularism, the civil rights movement, sexual liberation, gay rights and feminism since the 1960s. These conservative groups saw themselves as the norm, threatened by an alien cultural invasion associated with liberal permissiveness. 'Normative Americans prized hard work, personal responsibility, individual merit, delayed gratification, social mobility and other values that middle-class Whites recognized as their own'. Conservatives organized and reacted to greater inclusivity by declaring that these values were under threat, 'and caused this friction,' wrote Andrew Hartman.[15]

Hunter had 'hoped that by calling attention to the dynamic' of America's incipient culture war, he would help the country 'come to terms with the unfolding conflict and, perhaps, defuse some of the tensions'.[16] He was to be sorely disappointed. Disagreements, 'over issues such as abortion, sexuality, family values and church-state relations' have since turned into 'long-term, deeply embedded and fundamental distinctions' between conservative and liberal tribes 'that go beyond our ability to reason about them'. Following the first

What is Culture War?

Black American Presidency of Barack Obama, America's simmering culture war 'found oxygen and fresh purpose in the 2016 campaign of President Donald Trump, who has been called America's pre-eminent cultural warrior'.[17]

Trump explicitly admired the vitriol of the UK's Brexit referendum. What was ostensibly a narrow margin of difference on a specific question quickly became a seemingly intractable divide between Leavers and Remainers, spurring the crystallisation of division on a host of broader issues, including immigration, sovereignty, historical imagination and identity. The divide that has since rendered British politics so toxic, and which would give Boris Johnson's Conservative Party such a large majority in 2019, was an inspiration for Trump. He did all he could to exacerbate similar tensions between conservatives and liberals in the USA, as an electoral strategy. Even COVID was turned into a culture war issue, 'rather than something we could collectively come together to solve.' The wearing or not of face masks became a signifier of liberal or conservative allegiance. The USA's culture war has exacerbated partisanship to such an extent that a repeatedly and blatantly lying President could encourage his supporters to try forcefully to reject the outcome of a free and fair presidential election by storming the Capitol, and yet still avoid disqualification from future office.

Issues that tended to divide people in contingent ways become, in a culture war like that of the USA, fundamental questions of identity and spectres of existential threat. 'Politics becomes a proxy for cultural positions that simply won't brook any kind of dissent or argument ... The very idea of treating your opponents with civility is a betrayal. How can you be civil to people who threaten your very existence?'[18]

Deny & Disavow

The rise of social media has made it more difficult to engage with those who disagree on particular issues in the more equable ways that we might if we met them in person. Trump became the master of narcissistic, spiteful, childish and bullying tweets, lapped up by millions of followers until he was denied access to the platform (only to be reinstated after Elon Musk's takeover of Twitter in 2022). As Hunter puts it in the USA, 'our public culture is more polarized than we, as a people, are'. Social media multiplies the 'anonymity, the extremism of rhetoric, the absence of any kind of accountability in our public speech. They take what is already a shallow discourse — you know, the trading of slogans, and the like — and make it even more difficult to find any kind of depth'. As we will see, I have certainly found this to be the case in my attempts to debate imperial history with members of the History Reclaimed group.

Increasing inequalities have also played a key role in the success of the conservatives promoting culture war in the USA. The global recession caused by the banking crisis of 2008 'drove a wedge between the middle and lower-middle or working class and the highly trained, professionally educated managers, technocrats and intellectuals — basically, between the top 20 percent and the bottom 80 percent. And that meant [there] were now class differences that were overlaid upon some of these cultural differences ... In 2016, the single most important factor in determining a Trump vote was not having a college degree'.[19] Culture warriors in politics and the press tend to be privileged individuals, but they seek to fuel and channel a sense of injustice among those who can feel 'left behind' by a supposedly cosmopolitan, 'woke' elite.[20]

Populists fan the flames of resentment, but do their best to misdirect them. They are succeeding to a greater extent

What is Culture War?

in the USA and Europe than at any time since the Second World War. Those fuelling the USA's culture war share an underlying and deeply irrational fear of racial extinction in particular, which makes anti-racist movements and immigrants key targets for fear and loathing. Trump's slogan of Make America Great Again was 'a powerful call to restore "normative [White] America" as the nation stands at the brink of historic demographic change, with Whites expected to be a minority in the U.S. in 25 years, according to census projections'.[21] As the *Guardian*'s Jonathan Freedland puts it, 'to avert demography, many Republicans are willing to sacrifice democracy'.[22]

The USA's deep-rooted racial antagonism is an outcome of its history as a set of British Colonies, many of them formerly reliant on enslaved labour supplied by the Royal African Company. White fear of enslaved people's potential for retributive violence has informed conservative attitudes to African Americans long after US independence and the eventual abolition of slavery itself. This inter-generational fear, along with the prevalence of guns, is what lays behind the staggeringly high rate of police killing of African American men, including George Floyd. It is also the context for the development of Critical Race Theory — an attempt by pioneering African-American legal scholars in the 1990s to understand why USA's legal constitution retained systemically racist outcomes long after the abolition of Jim Crow laws and the achievements of the Civil Rights movement.

From 2020 the Republican-supporting commentator Christopher Rufo started a campaign to associate Critical Race Theory with Black Lives Matter and indeed any form of antiracism in the USA. As Benjamin Wallace-Wells explained in *The New Yorker*, Rufo thought that the debates over critical race theory offered a way for conservatives to 'take some ... essentially corrupted state agencies and then contest them, and then create rival power centers within them.' Because of some links with Marxist, among other influences, and because it could be made to seem like a personal attack on White people, 'Critical race theory is the perfect villain,' he wrote. With the trans-Atlantic transfer of conservative backlash strategies, the British right wing press now, quite absurdly, accuses anyone writing critically of the British Empire or campaigning against racism, of being influenced by Critical Race Theory. [23]

The most notable difference in the histories of slavery in the USA and the UK is that of distancing. Britons supplied enslaved people to colonies in what became the USA, the Caribbean and Central America, and tens of thousands of Britons up and down the social hierarchy owned enslaved people in these places without ever encountering them. They tended not to bring that many enslaved people to Britain itself. Despite this key difference with the USA, the determination with which culture warriors are resisting the inclusion of Black Britons' heritage in our 'national story', and not just those with ancestry in the Caribbean, but from all around the former empire, suggests that here too race is a potent dividing line. British culture warriors want to emulate 'Trump's ... genius [in] understanding the resentments of coming out on the losing side of global capitalism' and his ability to direct it not at the multimillionaire beneficiaries like himself, but at the liberal values of the middle classes — those whose sensitivities towards race and gender are supposedly betraying the nation — and at Black Lives Matter as a campaign directly representing the interests of Black people.

While Trump was inspired by Brexit, key figures in pro-Brexit UK politics have been inspired in turn by

What is Culture War?

him. One of them is the relatively obscure but influential Munira Mirza. Boris Johnson appointed Mirza as Director of the Number 10 Policy Unit in July 2019. She was, in Johnson's own approving words, 'ruthless.' During her career she moved from being an adherent of communism to a position on the more extreme populist wing of the Conservative Party. As Nick Cohen notes, 'When it failed to end imperialism and capitalism', the Revolutionary Communist Party 'ditched revolutionary politics but kept the absolute contempt for liberalism, labourism and human rights.' Mirza has described the anti-racism movement as a 'bogus moral crusade' imported from the US, '... with its demented campus dramas and neuroses about "safe spaces", "micro-aggressions" and "cultural appropriation".'[24] Before she resigned in the midst of Boris Johnson's 'partygate' scandal, she helped to mastermind the post-BLM culture war backlash.

The first part of this book begins by using a walking tour of Westminster's statues as an initial guide to the geography of the British Empire, how it was governed and how it related to racial violence. Part Two outlines four arenas in which populists, aided by Johnson's government, attempted to create culture war battlefields involving the history of Empire. They opened fronts in Parliament, the Commission on Race and Ethic Disparities (CRED), heritage and academia. I take each of these arenas in turn and examine the ways that Empire features in them. In Part Three, I try to identify things that are not generally taught to British schoolchildren, but which ought to be more widely known before the value judgements fuelling any putative UK culture war are made. The conclusion suggests answers to some of the tendentious points about the British Empire most frequently disseminated by conservative culture warriors in the media and articulated by their audiences.

Deny & Disavow

A Grade II-listed bronze statue of Robert Clive, 1st Baron Clive, by John Tweed, stands in King Charles Street, Whitehall, London. The work was unveiled in 1912 outside Gwydyr House, also in Whitehall, and was moved to its current location in 1916. Author's Photograph.

Chapter One

Walking Westminster

Seacole and Clive

Since Colston was toppled in Bristol our landscape of public memorialisation has been turned into a battlefield of the attempted culture war. Statues around the country have become the subjects of historical conversations of a kind that have never happened before. In many towns and cities statues are now being debated and reassessed at local level and the public awareness of historical debate over the Empire is growing as a result.[25]

I have been spending more time than I'd like in St Thomas' Hospital lately. St Thomas' is at the centre of Britain's memorial landscape, just across Westminster Bridge from the Houses of Parliament. Thanks to the events of the last few years I have become more aware of London's imperial statuary on my periodic walks to escape the wards. A walking tour around Westminster (with a diversion to Oxford) helps to orient ourselves to some of the key personalities and places of British imperial rule.

Deny & Disavow

The Guy's and St Thomas' NHS Foundation Trust has recently removed the statue of Sir Robert Clayton, President and renovator of St Thomas', and, like Colston, a major shareholder in the slave-trading Royal African Company.[26] Upon leaving St Thomas' main entrance, the first statue I encounter bucks the trend of White imperial men. In 2016, the memorial of Mary Seacole was erected in a small garden in the hospital grounds.[27] Despite the addition of the woman voted Greatest Black Briton to the National Curriculum, most Britons' schooling has left them in profound ignorance of the realities of Britain's imperial rule and its implications for Black subjects like Seacole. A cynical interpretation would see Seacole as a relatively comforting Black figure for inclusion in what imperial apologists like to think of as 'our shared national story'. She determinedly surmounted the racism of the Victorian Establishment but did so to aid British troops fighting an imperial war against Russia in the Crimea. Even if it is ameliorative rather than transformative of conventional views of Empire, the addition of Seacole's statue, like those of Mandela (2007) and Gandhi (2015) in Parliament Square is, in my opinion, still a good thing.

Seacole, Mandela and Gandhi are not alone, of course. There is a memorial landscape of Black people's experiences in London that is now gaining increased attention.[28] However, there are still many figures of the White male imperial sort littering the streets around the hospital. These statues are a continual reminder that Empire enabled White Britons 'to imagine themselves as both a race of masters and a master race'.[29]

The first thing I note after leaving the hospital and crossing Westminster Bridge to the heart of London's memorial landscape is the dates of most statues' erection. Victorian Britons professed an aversion to the 'tawdry glitter' of other European

Walking Westminster: Seacole and Clive

empires. In the 1870s Prime Minister Disraeli acceded only reluctantly to Queen Victoria's request for the title 'Empress', fearing accusations of being un-British. Just as the statues of Confederate generals now being pulled down in the southern states of the USA were built well after the Civil War, our statues of imperial men were often erected mainly after the period when Britons were most complacent about their global power.

In the USA, Confederate statues were initially erected when post-Civil War Reconstruction briefly threatened to unseat White Supremacy in the South, and then again when the twentieth century civil rights movement brought it into question. They were a re-assertion of White dominance during moments when it was felt to be newly imperilled. Most of the statues in Westminster date from the end of the Victorian and the Edwardian periods when the British Empire was facing new challenges from American and European rivals and mounting anticolonial resistance. This came mainly from indigenous elites, educated by the British and expecting to share in White people's privileges, but still denied equal status due to their race. Both the South African Native National Congress (later ANC) in South Africa and the Indian National Congress were formed by educated colonised elites to agitate for a share of White colonists' privileges. The SANNC's first campaign was for middle class, educated Africans to be allowed in White only train carriages, but these indigenous elites also requested a greater share in the governance of their own countries. Britons sculpted their imperial figures not in triumphal self-congratulation, but in a desperate gesture of reclamation of their exclusive right to rule in the face of such challenges. In more than one sense, now that I've opened my eyes to them, I can't stop seeing petrified imperial men all around Westminster.

The statue of Mary Seacole stands in the grounds of St Thomas' Hospital, Lambeth, London. Sculpted by Martin Jennings, the statue was erected in 2016. Author's photograph.

When protestors pulled down Colston's statue they drew attention to the distancing and disavowal of violence against people of colour that is generally inscribed in this late imperial British memorial-scape. Colston and others 'traded' people marked by a difference of phenotype as if

Walking Westminster: Seacole and Clive

they were commodities. As those defending the Empire like to point out, Africans too were extensively involved in the capture and trading of other Africans, but they tend not to stand on pedestals in British towns and cities.

The slave-owning system that Colston and other Britons scaled up from the seventeenth to the early nineteenth centuries relied upon markers of physical difference — on Blackness as a proxy for inferiority. But it wasn't just the transatlantic trade in people that was characterised by this difference. Once relocated on colonial plantations in the Americas and the Caribbean, colonial authorities could police the mobility and behaviour of the unfree much more efficiently if they were generally distinguished in appearance from the free. As the historian of slavey James Walvin explains, 'unlike other slave systems in the past (and later), slavery in the Americas was completely racialized. Only black people could be slaves; to be black was [overwhelmingly] to be enslaved, and to be enslaved was to be uniquely unequal and disadvantaged'.[30] This was why slavery was such a powerful contribution to a systemic imperial racism that long outlived emancipation, and which spread far beyond the Caribbean during the nineteenth century — the post-abolition period mainly celebrated in the statuary of Westminster.

By and large, the markers of difference between free and unfree in the slave colonies became those between planter and labourer, master and servant, citizen and subject, colonist and colonised around the British Empire as it expanded and reoriented to the east and south, conquering, subduing and colonizing people of colour in the aftermath of abolition.[31] The trump card of conservative culture warriors — 'OK Britain, like everyone else, had a role in slavery, but it was Britain that abolished it' — either totally ignores this long imperial after-life of rule by race, or extrapolates from exceptions such as the piecemeal and reluctant concessions to Indian elites at the beginning of the twentieth century.

Clive and India

Once across Westminster Bridge and around St James' Park, the most imposing statue is of Robert Clive, the East India Company officer who helped Britons and their Indian partners to reap dividends from other Indians, first through outright plunder and, in the longer term, through the extortion of rent. William Dalrymple writes that 'this statue stands as a daily challenge to every British person whose grandparents came from the former colonies'.[32]

Clive and his employer, the East India Company, were the beneficiaries of the collapse of Mughal imperial power in India from the 1740s. Clive began his career as a clerk for the East India Company in Madras, one of the three main bases, later presidencies, through which the Company would come to rule ever greater swathes of India. Founded in 1600, the Company was financed in the late eighteenth century by shareholders who represented some of Britain's wealthiest and highest status families. It used its bases in Madras (Chennai), Bombay (Mumbai) and Calcutta (Kolkata) to procure local goods for export but capitalised on the vacuum of centralised power as the Mughal Empire waned and disparate, regionally based Indian authorities contended for influence. This relatively chaotic political situation was further complicated by the overspill of Britain's warfare against France in India.

Clive joined the Company's Madras army, comprised of Indian recruits under British officers, during the wars against the French in India, earning a reputation as a capable commander. A spell as commissary gave a kickstart to his project of amassing personal wealth, whilst

Walking Westminster: Seacole and Clive

simultaneously pursuing Company interests. In 1756, the young nawab of Bengal, Siraj ud-Daula's seizure of the city of Calcutta, including the company base, Fort William, gave Clive an opportunity to extend those interests exponentially.

Siraj ud-Daula had become concerned about increasing European encroachment on his sovereignty as the Company expanded its presence and authority in Calcutta. When he imprisoned British captives in a cramped and stifling room overnight, allowing over forty of them to die, he inadvertently created the British legend of the 'Black Hole of Calcutta'. Clive led the avenging army which not only secured the Company's base in Calcutta but extracted reparations and new privileges from the nawab. He sensed an opportunity to push things further, though, when he joined a conspiracy among some of the nawab's followers to remove and replace him.

This development offered the prospect of intervening to secure a new, collaborating, nawab and open the whole of Bengal to Company influence. Clive began discussions with a potential candidate for the role — Mir Jafar, a general in the nawab's army. When Clive's and the nawab's troops confronted one another at the Battle of Plassey in 1757, a substantial portion of the nawab's army deserted him. The victorious Clive replaced Siraj ud-Daula with Mir Jafir, reporting to the Company's directors in London that 'this great revolution, so happily brought about, seems complete in every respect'. The Company gained a new revenue stream, most immediately with trade access to the whole of Bengal, and in the longer term by assuming the diwani, or right to collect revenue through taxation. Indian intermediaries thereafter collected rent from the regions' farming inhabitants on behalf of the Company's British shareholders. Clive became governor of

Deny & Disavow

Calcutta, effectively directing Mir Jafar in the governance of Bengal. He described his mission as 'Bullying and Keeping under the black fellows'.[33]

Clive's personal reward was substantial. Mir Jafar gifted him with presents worth £234,000 (worth roughly £23,400,000 today). Two years later, when Clive helped the newly installed nawab defend Bengal from the Mughal emperor's son, he was given land which drew revenue of around £27,000 (£2,700,000) a year from the taxation of its occupants. Such personal wealth encouraged other Britons to follow in Clive's footsteps. The trend took on something of the character of the later gold rushes. It initiated the plunder of India on a scale which caused scandal in late eighteenth century Britain, as a new class of Company 'nabobs' (from the Persian 'nawab') built country houses and acquired parliamentary seats, starting the transformation of Britain with the wealth extracted from Indians.[34]

After a spell as an MP, Shropshire landowner and military celebrity at home in the late 1750s, Clive went back to India in the mid-1760s, by which time the Company was continuing to diversify from trade into land acquisition and governance. The company acquired the right to collect revenue in the former Mughal provinces of Bihar and Orissa as well as Bengal, in return for military support and a 'tribute' payment to the Mughal emperor in Delhi, whose authority was now almost nominal.

The rent from the Company's Indian subjects that wasn't sent home as shareholder dividends was invested mainly in trade and in further strengthening the Company's armies, so that they could either overthrow more Indian rulers or provide a military backup for Company Resident Agents 'advising' those rulers. By the time Clive retired to England, he had a fortune of over £400,000 (£40,000,000) and was

Walking Westminster: Seacole and Clive

able to invest in estates and country houses at Claremont in Surrey and Oakly Park and the Okehampton estate in Devon as well as his existing lands in Shropshire. His collection of treasures from India is now on display at Powis castle, a National Trust property acquired by his son through marriage.[35]

Clive was by no means a universally popular figure. Both he and the Company were mired in controversies over the extortion of Indians who were now British subjects thanks to Company rule. The Bengal famine of 1769–70, which killed at least 1.2 million of these subjects (some estimates are as high as 10 million), raised particular concern about the nature of the company's business model. When the failure of the monsoon triggered initial food shortages, the Company's Governor General in Bengal, Warren Hastings admitted, 'It was naturally to be expected that the diminution of the revenue [tax collection] should have kept an equal pace with the other consequences of so great a calamity; that it did not was owing to its being violently kept up to its former standard.' Indeed, the Company went further, raising Indians' rent to maintain its own revenue, regardless of the impact on those trying to buy food at inflated prices. As the famine approached its peak, in April 1770, the Company added 10 percent to the land tax of the ensuing year whilst continuing to deny any responsibility for alleviating the grain shortage. When accused of instituting a system of ruthless plunder, Clive declared, 'Mr Chairman, at this moment I stand astonished at my own moderation!'[36]

In 1774, after withdrawing from a game of cards with friends, Clive was found dead in an adjoining room with a penknife in his throat. Most biographers suggest that he took his own life, having already attempted suicide twice as a younger man. He had been plagued by gout, and was in disgrace as 'Lord Vulture, the monstrous embodiment of all that was most corrupt and unprincipled about the East India Company'. Samuel Johnson wrote that he 'had acquired his fortune by such crimes that his consciousness of them impelled him to cut his own throat'.[37]

The fact that Clive was controversial in his own lifetime, however, was no bar to Sir William Forwood's determination to get his statue erected in Westminster in 1907, over 130 years after his death. By then, the historian Thomas Babington Macaulay had popularised a different version of Clive: not as the plunderer of India, but as the founder of a civilising British India. The Viceroy of India, Lord Curzon, backed the campaign to raise funds for matching statues in Britain and India. Despite Curzon's successor feeling that an Indian statue would be 'needlessly provocative', both were erected.[38] It is not only Dalrymple who decries the success of Forwood's early twentieth century campaign. Nick Robins, author of an excellent history of the East India Company, noted that 'the fact that one of Britain's greatest corporate rogues continues to have pride of place at the heart of government suggests that the British elite has not yet confronted its corporate and imperial past,' and called for the statue to be removed to a museum. There is now a twitter account dedicated to its removal.[39]

When Clive embarked the East India Company on its alternative income-generation pathway of taxing Indians, he could not have foreseen that, in 1833, the government would prevent it from pursuing further commerce entirely. Parliament, however, guaranteed its shareholders continued dividends of 10.5%. From then until the Company's dissolution, their income was drawn almost entirely from the rent charged to Indians for the privilege of being governed by its

Walking Westminster: Seacole and Clive

British shareholders. Macaulay, at the time Secretary to the Board of Control that oversaw the Company on behalf of government, justified the continued rule of India by shareholders in London. 'In Europe', he declared, 'the people are ... perfectly ... competent to hold some share of political power', but 'In India, you cannot have representative institutions'.[40]

The Company continued its ruthless rent extraction throughout subsequent famines, including that of 1837–8 which killed 800,000 British Indian subjects — the same number, incidentally, that were simultaneously freed from slavery in the Caribbean. It underwrote the building of railways, to serve British military and commercial purposes, from the 1840s. It continued under the guise of the Raj, which succeeded the Company after 1857, and it further continued during the famine, which killed another 5 million British Indian subjects in 1878–9. More broadly, an increasing share of domestic expenditure within the UK, as well as the expenses for governing the Empire, were covered by taxation levied on colonial subjects of colour who had no say in government.[41]

Chapter Two

Wolseley

Leaving Clive behind, the next statue comes into view as I wander into Horse Guards Parade, and it leads my thoughts from India to other parts of the Empire — parts that have been relatively neglected in the culture war, where India has come so often to stand for the Empire as a whole.

Sir Garnet Wolseley and the Expansion of Empire

Field Marshal Sir Garnet Wolseley was the inspiration for Gilbert and Sullivan's 'very model of a modern Major-general', satirically lauded for his achievements in science and mathematics but supposedly lacking in military nous. In fact, he was one of the most effective military commanders in the history of the British Empire. Erected in 1920, again as a mark of threatened imperial sway, the plaque underneath his horse indicates the diverse sites of his military exploits: 'Burmah 1852–3, Crimea 1854–5, Indian Mutiny 1857–9, China 1860–1, Red River 1870, Ashanti 1873–4, South Africa 1879, Egypt 1882, Soudan 1884–5.' Following his trajectory around the Empire enables us to view a sample of the violence that imperial expansion entailed.

If Clive helped secure India for the British Empire, Wolseley was the pre-eminent conqueror of territory

Sir Garnet Wolseley and the Expansion of Empire

elsewhere during the second half of the nineteenth century. He exerted his influence directly, but also through a tight-knit group of generals who benefitted from his patronage. Known as the Wolseley 'ring' or 'gang', these men, including John McNeill, William Butler, Redvers Buller, Hugh McCalmont, Henry Brackenbury, John Maurice, George Colley, Baker Russell and Henry Evelyn Wood, monopolised Victorian campaigns to conquer people of colour around the world, and to punish them for defying British demands. Wolseley's first campaign experience was the result of provocation by the expansionist East India Company, resulting in the annexation of Lower Burma. After the Crimean campaign, designed to shore up the Ottoman Empire against a Russian empire that threatened British control of India, Wolseley joined the army led by Sir Colin Campbell, which relieved the siege of Lucknow and brutally suppressed the 1857 Indian Uprising against Company rule.

In Britain, the rebellion of 1857 is popularly held to have been almost exclusively a mutiny of Indian sepoys, soldiers in the East India Company's army — in this case the Bengal army. The stock explanation is that their religious sensibilities were offended by the introduction of new ammunition cartridges. These were greased with the fat of cows, sacred for Hindus, and pigs, offensive to Muslims. Even the appellation 'Indian Mutiny', rather than Uprising, commonly used in Britain, implies that the violence was a solely military affair.

The immediate impetus for rebellion did indeed originate among sepoys and there had been previous mutinies confined largely within the Company's garrisons. The label 'Mutiny', however, elides the much broader rebellious coalition that developed in 1857 — one that was sustained for more than a year across a large swathe of northern India.

The equestrian statue of Garnet Wolseley, 1st Viscount Wolseley, is located at the Horse Guards Parade in London. It is by Sir William Goscombe John and was unveiled by the Duke of Connaught in 1920. Author's photograph.

The Uprising posed a far greater challenge to the British governance of India than a mere soldiers' mutiny.

The rebellion arose through an alliance of Company

soldiers, noblemen, clerics, artisans, local officials, minor landlords and peasants, excluded from the emerging unequal Company partnership with Indian merchant elites. These diverse groups shared an alienation from British rule that had been mounting for well over a decade. It was the result of their exclusion from decision-making, the Company's insistence on White Britons' innate superiority and its treatment of Indians, regardless of their relative status, with 'contempt'.[42]

Lord Dalhousie, the governor general appointed by the Company Directors to rule India from Calcutta in 1848, shared a considerable part of the responsibility. Dalhousie had been friends with William Gladstone when they studied at Christ Church College Oxford. Neither of these men was plagued by self-doubt. Dalhousie admitted 'We certainly are immensely cocky but then, hang it, we have reason'.[43] As a former President of the Board of Trade, he had overseen the British Government's response to 'railway mania'. This inspired his subsequent enthusiasm for railway building in India, the difference being that there he was 'freed from the limitations imposed by the parliamentary system' and therefore 'able to achieve his own ideal of central railway planning and control.'[44] His mission was to extend Company authority over as much of India as possible.

In 1853, Dalhousie's 216-page handwritten 'memorandum' encouraged further investment in India's railways on the grounds that they would propel British enterprise, increase production, and allow the exploitation of India's coal and minerals.[45] Above all they would enable the Company's officials and soldiers to traverse India's terrain more effectively, spearheading the subcontinent's broader transformation. The trick was to mitigate the risk for investors by guaranteeing minimum returns, derived from the taxation of Indians. As the lobbyist Hyde Clark put it, the intention was to 'make the Hindoos form the railways and enable us [Britons] to reap a large portion of the profits'.[46]

By the beginning of 1857, the Company was guaranteeing a five per cent return for railway investors in India — not much compared to the returns that investors in railways gained elsewhere, for example in South America, but enough to raise the necessary finance. The Madras Presidency had opened its first line in 1856 and in Bombay, 50,000 Indian labourers were paying a heavy price for the ambitious engineering required to run a railway through the Western Ghats. A British engineer's report complained that as soon as the monsoonal weather was optimal for construction, 'fatal epidemics, such as cholera and fever ... break out and the labourers are generally of such feeble constitution, and so badly provided with shelter and clothing, that they speedily succumb to those diseases and the benefits of the fine weather are, thereby, temporarily lost.'[47]

All this technological promise and excitement spurred on Dalhousie's plans. Under its 'doctrine of lapse' the Company was authorised to assume direct government of any independent Indian state where the heir's succession was disputed. Rarely invoked beforehand, Dalhousie saw it as key to a programme of massive territorial consolidation and investment. In an admission overlooked by today's defenders of British rule in India, he dismissed talk of annexations being for the immediate benefit of Indian subjects as 'nothing else than ambitious and hypothetical humbug'. The expansion of direct sovereignty was necessary to extend and tighten the Company's grip on the sub-continent, raise more revenue to invest in its 'modernization', and secure the returns that had been guaranteed to shareholders in Britain.[48]

Dalhousie committed the Company to take 'advantage of every just opportunity which presents itself for consolidating the territories which already belong to us, by taking possession of States which may lapse in the midst of them; for getting rid of those petty intervening principalities which may be a means of annoyance, but which can never, I venture to think, be a source of strength' for the company and Britain.[49] His programme of annexation began on a small scale with the princely state of Satara in 1848. Its Rajah complained to the Board of Control, that 'in the next Charter of the East India Company' it may as well be declared, that English morality is no more than a question of latitude and longitude; that in India ... what is virtue and what is vice, what is innocence and what guilt, what truth, what falsehood, shall be determined by the complexion of the agent; the white man ... being always regarded as the embodiment of virtue and truth, incapable of wrong ... and alone worthy of belief — the dark man, or native, held up as the personification of vice and falsehood ... to be condemned, degraded, vilified, punished, imprisoned at will, tortured, beggared.'[50]

Dalhousie did not need to invoke the doctrine of lapse when he annexed the Punjab the following year. Ranjit Singh's kingdom, a former ally of the Company, was conquered and taken under Company control when Duleep Singh, the young successor, was deposed. At the same time, Dalhousie took the Koh-i-Noor diamond, gaining favour by sending it to Queen Victoria.

The Punjab was the most formidable state to have been taken under Company control since the defeat of the Marathas. Its annexation entailed not just the overthrow of a dynasty but the extension of British rule over most Sikhs. Dalhousie recognised that 'until revenues mend' and the territory was pacified, Sikhs themselves would have to have a say in the running of their government alongside the British administrator, John Lawrence. Governing and taxing the former kingdom with a lighter touch than in other parts of India and encouraging Sikhs' recruitment into the Company army proved to be advantageous, since when the rebellion first broke out it was primarily Sikh troops who were deployed to hold it in check until British reinforcements could arrive.

In 1853 Dalhousie explained that the annexation of Nagpur alone 'added 40 lakhs of rupees to the company's annual revenue and 80,000 square miles of valuable territory in central India'. Jhansi, also absorbed in 1853, was too small to add much to the revenue, but 'since it lay in the midst of other British districts its possession ... would tend to the improvement of the general internal administration of British possessions'.[51] Just as worryingly for India's established elites and the Company's former allies, Dalhousie set about abolishing the titles and privileges of heirs to defunct sovereignties, just in case their persistence raised any doubts about the exclusivity of Company authority. It was such measures which denoted most clearly the shift in the Company's main alliance, from landed to mercantile interests, in the 1840s and 1850s. With the former threatened by the newly aggressive stance of the Company government, 'political integration secured integration of markets for commodities, capital, and labour, and closer union between internal trade and maritime trade' suited both merchant Indian elites and British Company shareholders.[52]

Dalhousie's intervention in Awadh proved an annexation too far. The Company had recognised this small Indian state centred on Lucknow and straddling the route from Bengal to the northwest frontier, as independent since 1801. Its nawabs had lent the Company funds to enable the

Sir Garnet Wolseley and the Expansion of Empire

invasion of Afghanistan in 1838 and some of its wealthier subjects even owned Company shares. About 40,000 sepoys from the kingdom were serving in the Company's Bengal army. Much as he tried, Dalhousie admitted that he could not 'find a pretext' for annexation under the doctrine of lapse. Instead, he instructed the Company's Resident Agent in the kingdom, James Outram, to prepare a report on misgovernment by its new nawab, Wajid Ali Shah. Outram portrayed the nawab as a 'sensuous lush' and recommended a more intrusive Company oversight.[53] Dalhousie however annexed the entire state. When the sepoys rebelled in 1857 recruits from Awadh were prominent among them.

Dalhousie is remembered in Britain as the great moderniser of India due to his investments in rail, telegraph and schooling, but he also breached the partly coerced and partly negotiated understanding with the Indian nobility that had enabled the Company's relative power in the subcontinent during the 1830s. Up until the mid-1840s around a third of the subcontinent had still been governed by sovereigns who remained outside of Company control or who retained some independence under the supervision of a Company Resident. But 'in the eight years he was in charge, Dalhousie annexed more than any other single Governor-General, a quarter of a million square miles.'[54]

Dalhousie's incessant usurpation of Indian authorities, even if they had already accepted Company oversight, was what drove Indian nobles to rebel in 1857. But a much more profound and deeper intrusion into the lives of ordinary Indians motivated many more to turn on the British. The Company had come to be seen as a voracious and insatiable extractor of rent, regardless of the suffering that it inflicted on its Indian subjects.

Dalhousie's massive, underwritten investments in

railways and roads had not yet brought significant financial returns. By 1850, the Company's debt stood at £50 million, more than twice its annual income. 'The consequence was an effort to find additional sources of cash, and to do so by squeezing existing Indian(s)' as well as through annexing more territory from which to extract rent.[55] By 1857 land tax was being imposed at two thirds of the total produce in many north Indian villages. Indians of all social classes on the Indo-Gangetic plain were paying indirectly for British-built railways and British shareholder returns, whether or not they could afford or wanted them.

Almost as importantly, the elevated tax was being collected in new and alienating ways. In the 1830s aristocratic governors, zamindars and Muslim scholars across India's diverse patchwork of states had enjoyed some legitimacy in collecting local taxes. Whether they operated in princely states under Company oversight or on behalf of the Company itself in directly governed territories, these officials were embedded in the communities from which they drew revenue. They tended to be amenable to negotiation on rates and timings. They would waive rent on land for temples, schools and pilgrimage centres and award pensions to certain powerful individuals to secure their consent. The Company officials who had replaced them by 1857, however, understood and cared less about negotiated obligations and inherited arrangements. They had been trained at the Company's College at Haileybury in England and for them, rent was not a matter of negotiation, but a number to be determined formulaically. For most of the Company's Indian subjects, theirs 'was a strange way to govern a country'.[56]

The Company men who imposed the new taxes were inexplicably inflexible. They saw expenditure on religious symbolism as wastage rather than obligation, and they condemned the judicious waiving of rent as typically Indian corruption. More broadly, the imposition of alien laws and practices, even if intended by some officials ultimately to improve the condition of colonised subjects, was widely resented. In 1857, these impositions included initiatives to 'liberate' Indian women from violence at the hands of Indian men and enable their education. The Hindu Widows' Remarriage Act, in 1856, for instance, provided Hindu women and girls with legal safeguards against the loss of inheritance for remarrying but encountered fierce opposition from Indian men who considered it a flagrant breach of Hindu custom. Missionaries, officials and army officers' more concerted attempts to proselytise Christianity were just as provocative to many Indian men and women. Britons' conviction of moral superiority had rendered them oblivious to the resentment they were building.

The opportunity for such disparate groups to rebel came only when a significant proportion of the Company's own soldiers mutinied. This occurred, in essence, because Indian men's service in the Company's armies had turned from being a source of pride to one of shame.

During the wars of conquest in the late eighteenth and early nineteenth centuries, the Company's troops had come to think of themselves as an admired elite. Service with the army was a family tradition which guaranteed high status and pay. An early proclamation from the mutineers of 1857, both Hindu and Muslim, read 'It is we who have conquered the whole territory extending from Calcutta to Kabul for the English, because they did not bring any English army with them from England'.[57] However, Company officials seemed now to evidence little gratitude for these services. The Company had progressively undermined its Indian recruits' status well before the introduction of the greased cartridges proved a tipping point.

Dalhousie had abolished extra allowances for soldiers who served beyond the presidencies in which they had been recruited. His successor, Canning (whose statue stands adjacent to Parliament Square), then forced new recruits to fight overseas if the Company so ordered. This was despite the Company's understanding that passage over the sea could entail a loss of caste for Hindu soldiers.[58] Most fundamentally, the growing British determination to ensure social distance between themselves and their Indian subjects meant that sepoys too now found it more difficult to explain and negotiate their grievances. They 'had no means of protesting against what they might feel to be a foolish measure, or of giving public expression to their own wishes ... They misunderstood every act, and whatever law was passed was misconstrued by men who had no share in the framing of it, and hence no means of judging its spirit.'[59] Rumours that new cartridges were greased with polluting fat took root in this context of distrust and spread like wildfire in early 1857, whatever the Company did to try to allay concern.

To return to our statue tour now, British troops, among them the young Wolseley, killed hundreds of thousands of Indians in revenge for the atrocities committed by rebels, especially their massacre of 120 British women and children at Cawnpore. In October 1857, when news of Cawnpore dominated the British press, Charles Dickens summed up the British public's mood of vengeance: 'I wish I were the Commander in Chief in India .... I should do my utmost to exterminate the Race upon whom the stain of the late cruelties rested ... proceeding, with all convenient dispatch and merciful swiftness of execution, to blot it out of mankind and raze it off the face of the earth.'[60] British soldiers, many of whom shared Dickens' avenging sentiment, rounded up and shot or hanged civilians as they restored the Company's rule across northern India. They publicly executed captured rebels by blowing them apart after strapping them across the mouths of cannons.

Uncounted thousands of non-combatants were killed in Delhi after its recapture. General Roberts, whose equestrian statue neighbours Wolseley's on Horse Guards Parade, described the march through the former Mughal capital 'in the early morning light' after its recapture as 'a gruesome proceeding. Our way from the Lahore gate by the Chandni Chauk led through a veritable city of the dead; not a sound was to be heard but the falling of our own footsteps; not a living creature was to be seen. Dead bodies were strewn about in all directions, in every attitude that the death-struggle had caused them to assume, and in every stage of decomposition.'[61]

Opium Wars

Three years after Wolseley was in India helping to suppress the Uprising, he was in China, helping to enforce the illegal importation of Indian-grown opium. This brings us to the East India Company's third major revenue stream after trade and rent extraction: narcotics smuggling. By the 1830s, the East India Company had perfected a drugs industry, obliging its tenants in parts of northern India and Bengal to grow opium poppies and remit them to Company agents, who supervised their manufacture. Private companies like Jardine Matheson infiltrated the prohibited opium into China through Canton, where officials turned a blind eye. However, the Qing Emperor was getting serious about suppressing the trade that undermined his authority. In December 1838, a new Cantonese governor, Lin, had threatened to attack British clippers from India unless all the opium on the coast was surrendered. William Jardine, director of the most prolific smuggling company, Jardine Matheson, complained 'Not an opium pipe [was] to be seen, not a retail vendor . . . not a single enquiry after the drug'. He and his associates set off to London to lobby for war.

In 1839 Lin destroyed £4 million worth of Company opium. John Cam Hobhouse, head of the Board of Control, asserted that, in declaring war, 'England was not pursuing purely selfish trade ambitions; rather she was fighting for the opening of trade for all nations.' The new steamship *Nemesis* led the assault, resulting in the humiliation of the Qing dynasty, the forced opening of the opium trade through Chinese ports and the seizure of Hong Kong.

This was only the first of two Opium Wars waged by Britain against China, though. Wolseley fought in the second of them, provoked by the British consul in Canton and Prime Minister Palmerston, whose statue is also in Parliament Square.

Along with British manufacturers and merchants, Palmerston felt that not enough had been exacted from China after the First Opium War nearly twenty years beforehand. With a foothold secured for other British interests in that war, British manufacturers and merchants were pressing the government to prize open China's vast but protected market, and to push for further concessions for the opium trade, including its legalization throughout China (even though it was still banned in Britain).[62]

In October 1856, Henry Parkes, the British consul in Canton, and John Bowring, the plenipotentiary in China and Governor of Hong Kong, confected a major crisis out of

Sir Garnet Wolseley and the Expansion of Empire

The steamship HMS *Nemesis* destroying Chinese war junks in 1841.

a minor incident. The Qing Governor in Canton, Yeh, had seized the *Arrow*, a ship moored on the river, because two of its crew had been identified as pirates. Mistakenly believing that the vessel was still registered as British, Parkes had stormed aboard the ship where the men were being held to demand their release, only to be repulsed by the Qing guard. Insulted, the consul appealed to Bowring, alleging that sailors under British protection had been arrested, and that Britain's Red Ensign flag had been torn down during the arrest of the crew.

Parkes and Bowring discovered within a day or two that the *Arrow*'s British registration had in fact lapsed. They also knew that it was highly unlikely that the British flag had been flying on the vessel whilst it lay in port, never mind torn down and insulted. It was the custom for all ships to lower flags in port and neutral witnesses testified that the

Deny & Disavow

Arrow had been flying no flag when boarded. Yet the British officials continued to force the issue as a major diplomatic incident. Seeing the two British diplomats' harrying as an inconvenient distraction from the massive trauma of the ongoing Taiping Rebellion engulfing much of China, Yeh agreed to hand over all the captured crew members.

Bowring and Parkes then escalated their demands. They ordered that Yeh's residency complex be shelled by British warships every ten minutes until he publicly humbled himself before them and allowed them access to the forbidden walled city beyond the port. Palmerston now had his chance to force a renegotiation of the treaty which had brought the First Opium War to a close. He ordered a dossier of Bowring's justifications for attacking Canton to be published to garner support for war. Unfortunately for him, many MPs, including those in his own Liberal party, saw the *Arrow* affair as a shameful and bullying attempt to humiliate the Qing authorities on the flimsiest of pretexts. Lord Lyndhurst asked 'Was there ever conduct more abominable, more flagrant, in which … more false pretence has been put forward by a public man in the service of the British government?'[63]

Palmerston was at least honest in pointing out that the opium trade, no matter how unsavoury it was, helped to balance Britain's trade deficit with China. The trade would have to be legalized and the Chinese interior opened whether the Qing authorities liked it or not. Nonetheless, he claimed, the insult to the British flag on the *Arrow* was a *casus belli* in its own right. In a foretaste of the current government's 'war on woke', Palmerston declared that the problem with those who criticized war on China was that 'Everything that was English was wrong, and everything that was hostile to England was right'.[64] Finding that he had

Sir Garnet Wolseley and the Expansion of Empire

insufficient support among MPs, Palmerston announced the dissolution of Parliament and called a general election. The Prime Minister had sensed that the critical MPs were out of touch with their constituents on the issue, just as Boris Johnson did when dissolving parliament for the 2019 'Get Brexit Done' election. Amid complaints of creating an 'artificial public opinion', Palmerston solicited the cartoonist George Cruikshank to sway the electorate by circulating images of Qing methods of torture and execution. The Prime Minister himself lied repeatedly that British heads had been displayed on the walls of Canton.

Palmerston issued a written address which was printed in *The Times* and other evening newspapers and distributed as a flyer across Britain. Despite his knowledge that the *Arrow* was no longer registered British, it began, 'An insolent barbarian, wielding authority at Canton, had violated the British flag, broken the engagements of treaties, offered rewards for the heads of British subjects in that part of China, and planned their destruction by murder, assassinations, and poisons'. With what the diarist Charles Greville called 'enormous and shameful lying', Palmerston won a landslide victory in the general election that April. Many of his opponents lost their seats. All thanks, the *Daily News* claimed, to 'the excited ignorance of a misinformed public'. *Reynolds's Newspaper* lamented, 'What a truly melancholy exhibition! The foremost nation of all the Old World rushing, and screaming, and swearing, and shouting in mad hysterical hallelujahs, the praises of a man whose principal characteristic was an unconquerable disposition to jest at national calamities, and whose greatest recommendation was a species of boasts'.[65]

In alliance with the French and with informal American help, British forces humiliated the Qing armies once again in Palmerston's populist war, and Wolseley earned his spurs as a young commander in the conflict. Having helped secure the lucrative narcotics trade and enforced British imports to China, he participated in the looting of Beijing's Imperial Summer Palace. Charles Gordon, whom Wolseley would later try to save from a famously stoic death in Khartoum, complained that 'These palaces were so large & we were so pressed for time that we could not plunder carefully'.[66]

Confederation Wars

After his participation, in quick succession, in the conflicts in India and China, the British imperial policy which did most to shape Wolseley's subsequent impact on the world was Confederation. It was pursued by Lord Carnarvon, Secretary of State for the Colonies, after the shock of the Indian Uprising had prompted the more integrated governance of the disparate and fragmented empire from the current Foreign Office building. The rationale for the policy was outlined in Charles Dilke's popular book *Greater Britain*. Dilke's theme, unashamedly, was 'the grandeur of our race, already girding the earth, which it is destined, perhaps, eventually to overspread'. Dilke was frank that the 'defeat of the cheaper by the dearer peoples' was an essential precondition for this spread of British civilization.[67]

Carnarvon's first step was the confederation of the separate colonies in Canada, so that they could form a better administered and more prosperous whole within this Greater Britain. In 1869, however, Métis people of mixed First Nations and French colonial descent, recognised as aboriginal to Canada, established an independent government of their own at the Red River Colony, in today's Manitoba. The Métis declared their intention of joining the Canadian federation planned by the Colonial

Sir Garnet Wolseley and the Expansion of Empire

Office in London, but on their own terms: representation in Parliament, a bilingual legislature and chief justice, and recognition of their land claims.

Wolseley was charged with putting down the Métis 'rebellion' after an opponent of their leader, Louis Riel, was killed. Having led an expedition that was a logistical marvel, involving portage of boats between waterways across over 500 miles of difficult terrain, Wolseley arrived at the Métis base at Fort Garry too late to capture any rebels. But his show of force succeeded in suppressing the most viable attempt by aboriginal people to have their interests represented in a united British Canada.

After the Red River Expedition, Wolseley's reputation soared in Britain. He became trouble-shooter in chief for the Empire. If independent-minded people of colour blocked aspirations for a Greater Britain, represented by Dilke's notion of Anglo-Saxon dominance across the globe, Wolseley was the man either to subdue them or to lead an expedition to punish them. His next campaign was against the Asante kingdom. In 1872, the Colonial Office was seeking to consolidate Britain's scattered governmental entities on the West African coast, in accord with the larger objective of confederation in the settler colonies. This included the purchase of the Dutch Gold Coast with its port of Elmina, and its incorporation within the British Gold Coast colony. However, Elmina was also the coastal trade outlet for the Asante, a kingdom whose wealth and power, like Britain's, had been built in part through slave trading. In early 1873 Kofi Karikari, the Asante king, ordered his army to attack the British and reclaim the port.

Wolseley's retaliatory expedition, including Black West Indian troops and Fante allies, destroyed the Asante capital Kumasi, burning down villages as it went. The expedition was justified in Britain as an attempt to end Asante practices of slavery but used enslaved women among its 17,000 porters. The official haul of plunder from Kumasi included King Kofi's state umbrella and a golden stool, which Wolseley gave to Queen Victoria. Wolseley had drawn up guidelines on the distribution of plunder from British Army campaigns against 'uncivilised' (Black) enemies. Since the prize money from the Asante loot was considered too little to distribute among all the soldiers who participated, they were awarded an extra thirty days pay in lieu. Asante gold is now in the British Museum, the Wallace Collection; the Royal Artillery mess at Woolwich; the National Army Museum and the Green Jackets Regimental Museum, despite repeated calls for its return to Ghana.[68]

Wolseley brought the Asante kingdom under British 'protection' in one of roughly sixty 'small wars' fought by the British army against people of colour in the second half of the nineteenth century.[69] In a handbook for such campaigns written in 1896, Colonel Callwell defined them as being against 'savages', 'deficient in courage and provided with poor weapons.' Such wars, he wrote, were an inevitable 'epilogue to encroachments into lands beyond the confines of existing civilization … the great nation which seeks expansion in remote quarters of the globe must accept the consequences.'[70]

Having emerged victorious from Asante, Wolseley next joined the long running campaign to bring Southern Africa's diverse colonies, Boer republics and independent African kingdoms under confederated British rule, following the Canadian precedent. Here, his trajectory converged with that of the very next imperial man that I encountered on my Westminster statue walk, standing on a plinth on the Victoria Embankment, just along from the Houses of Parliament.

Sir Garnet Wolseley and the Expansion of Empire

Thomas Fowell Buxton's son Charles had also sought to revive waning British antislavery commitment, with a monument to his father's campaign first erected in Parliament Square in the 1850s. However, the local authority removed it in 1949, not because it symbolised anything objectionable, but because its gothic style did not fit with a classical re-design of the Square. In 1957, on 150th anniversary of the abolition of the slave trade, it was rebuilt, without its piped water and drinking cups, just along the riverbank from the Houses of Parliament. Author's photograph.

Chapter Three

Bartle Frere and Rhodes

Sir Henry Bartle Frere had come to southern Africa as High Commissioner, also determined to effect Confederation. His reputation was that of an antislavery man of action. After 1833 and the abolition of slavery in the British colonies in the Caribbean, the Cape and Mauritius (but not yet in India), Britons patted themselves on the back as the most benign exponents of imperial rule in history. But being anti-slavery did not mean that they were anticolonial or anti-racist. Far from discouraging further aggression against Africans, Britain's mantle as an antislavery nation encouraged it. It was not just Wolseley's assault on Kumasi that was justified as an anti-slavery intervention. As the historian Richard Huzzey explains, 'Anti-slavery traditions helped to translate private interest and personal ambitions into national interest and patriotic duty'.[71] Bartle Frere was in the forefront of this new, moral crusade.

Sir Henry Bartle Frere:
A Liberal Antislavery Activist Colonises Africa

Under Governor General Dalhousie, Bartle Frere had been the East India Company's Resident in Satara, one of the first states that Dalhousie had annexed. From there, Frere moved to Sind, where he installed a postal system based on Britain's, which was subsequently adopted across India. It is often proclaimed as one of the enduring, positive, legacies of British rule. As Governor of Bombay he again sponsored

Bartle Frere and Rhodes

modernizing, liberal projects, including the Deccan College at Pune, and a specialist college to instruct Indians in civil engineering.

Both a high churchman and a member of the Antislavery Society, Frere had long condemned what he called the 'fashion of looking down on all men who differed from us in colour or in race.' He also bemoaned the British public's general ignorance of the Arab-led East African slave trade. In March 1872, Frere invoked the original struggle of Thomas Fowell Buxton and his generation against British slavery in the Caribbean, exhorting 'the present supporters of the anti-slavery movement to imitate their predecessors and to be up and doing'.[72]

Aside from 'we abolished slavery' and 'what about the railways', the next most popular refrain of the culture war's imperial apologists is 'what about the Arab slave trade'. It was precisely this that Frere sought to draw to the attention of the British public in the early 1870s. Although much of this continuing Indian Ocean slave trade was financed by wealthy Indian merchants doing nicely out of the imperial trade networks centred on Bombay, British outrage was becoming focused on Zanzibar's sultan, Barghash bin Said. The Foreign Office feared that he was susceptible to mounting Islamist influence in the region.

In 1872 the Foreign Office asked Frere if he would put his antislavery campaigning to practical use as the new British envoy to the sultan. Exceeding his instructions, Frere ordered the Royal Navy to seize any slave ships sailing between Zanzibar and the African coast. He then threatened Barghash with a total blockade. The sultan was forced to close the slave market in Zanzibar, end the import and export of enslaved people, and ban British subjects, including Indians, from owning enslaved people. Arab slave owners, however, were left in possession of their human 'property'.

Deny & Disavow

By the late-1870s Bartle Frere had become a kind of civilian management consultant for the British Empire, just as Wolseley was its military trouble-shooter. Carnarvon, at the Colonial Office, now sent Frere to pursue confederation in southern Africa and the two men whose statues stand within a half mile of each other both ended up in South Africa. Whatever Bartle Frere thought about basic human equality and the immorality of slavery did not impede him launching a new and extremely violent phase in the conquest of Black southern African societies thereafter.

By the time Wolseley arrived in Natal in 1879, Bartle Frere had already attacked and defeated the Griqua, the Gcaleka Xhosa and the Zulu in a series of Callwell's 'small' wars of aggression. Wolseley was despatched when things were going badly after the British defeat by Zulu at Isandlwana, but he arrived too late to take command before Lord Chelmsford atoned for the defeat with a crushing victory aided by Gatling guns, at the Battle of Ulundi. Wolseley would have to content himself with finishing another 'small war' that Frere had launched and paused before the Zulu campaign — against the Pedi. Driven to seek sanctuary in rocky outcrops and caves, men, women and children were attacked and killed by Swazi allies and British troops until forced to acquiesce in British overrule.

In the meantime, Bartle Frere was formulating a scheme for the governance of the conquered Zulu which anticipated the family histories of some of our more prominent Conservative politicians. Prime Minister Rishi Sunak and former and current Home Secretaries Priti Patel and Suella Braverman are all descended from families that acquired a precarious status, subordinate to White settlers and officials, but elevated above African subjects, in the British colonies of southeast and East Africa.

Indian colonial intermediaries are most closely associated

Bartle Frere and Rhodes

The 1888 statue of Henry Bartle Frere is in Whitehall Gardens in London. It is by the sculptor Thomas Brock. Author's photograph.

with the colonies of Kenya and Uganda. Notoriously, the post-independence Ugandan dictator Idi Amin expelled some 80,000 Indian subjects in 1972. These communities took root mainly from the mid-1890s when labourers recruited to build the East African railway were followed by traders, police and administrators from India, but Bartle Frere had drawn up a scheme to employ Indian subjects in the management of the Zulu some twenty years beforehand. He was among the first imperial officials to argue that certain classes of Indians could serve as a buffer between relatively few white officials and a conquered, dispossessed mass of African subjects.

After the disaster of Isandlwana, Frere spent the time awaiting reinforcements from Britain planning for the postwar occupation of Zululand. What he had in mind reverted to his Indian experience and to the fact that thousands of Indians were already employed as indentured workers on Natal's sugar plantations. He requested that the Colonial Office mediate with the India Office and War Office to send him Indian soldiers — sepoys — to assist in the control of Zululand.

Frere wrote: 'There are objections of race and colour, which would be obstacles to an experiment anywhere but in the neighbourhood of Natal, where Indian Coolies are already present in considerable numbers; but Sepoys would probably be found very useful ... anywhere from the Kei northwards to the Limpopo ... When the strength of the Zulu Army is once broken, and the people relegated to their natural pastoral and agricultural avocations, it would take a very small force of Sepoys to keep 400,000 of them in order with the aid of a good Zulu police ... if any Indian authority would consider the force necessary to keep in order a million of men of the most martial races in India, he would probably name a garrison very much smaller than anything yet contemplated for Natal and Zululand combined'.

Once discharged, Frere continued, the imported sepoys could join the ranks of the indentured workers, and enhance the colony's trade, 'though a Madras Sepoy would probably find himself more at home at once among the Indian Coolies than Sepoys from other parts of India.' As

Bartle Frere and Rhodes

for the existing Indian population of the colony, 'that ... material is generally much inferior to the Indian Sepoy of the same race — the ordinary Sepoys are the finest of the population, while the ordinary coolies who emigrate, are often the poorest and weakest.'

Frere's scheme was stymied by the anticipated cost and the post-Isandlwana Colonial Office belief that superior White soldiers were needed against the formidable Zulu. I doubt that his plan for Zululand acted as a direct precedent for the later East African colonial administrations, but what it does highlight is the way in which Britain's imperial administrators thought of India as a resource not only of labour for other parts of the empire, but also of intermediaries to help them maintain control of other 'races'.

Tens of thousands of African people were killed in Frere's and Wolseley's unprovoked wars of South African confederation, and viable, independent societies were broken apart and families separated as the template for apartheid was laid. These were imperial wars, launched from London in pursuit of Greater Britain, with even the Cape Colony's parliament of overwhelmingly White representatives reluctant to incur the expense. The Cape colonial government would become a more aggressive entity again only once Cecil Rhodes, as we will see, started using it as his political base for the invasion of African territories to the north in the 1880s.

Wolseley's next war was waged to preserve control of the Empire's main strategic lifeline. Egypt was nominally an Ottoman territory but governed by a pasha who had become indebted to British and French financiers and governments. Its French-built Suez Canal played a vital role connecting Britain with India and the colonies of the southern hemisphere, so when Urabi Pasha, a soldier in the Pasha's army, led a rebellion against indirect Anglo-French control in 1882, the British government intervened. One of Urabi's demands was for an Egyptian parliament like the ones that liberal Britons demanded for themselves. His was a proto-nationalist rebellion which predated that of Nasser by some seventy years.

When pro- and anti-Urabi groups clashed in Alexandria and Europeans fled, the British response was to bombard the city's fortifications, with uncounted numbers of civilians killed by shelling of the streets around. Wolseley's troops then suppressed Urabi's revolt at the Battle of Tel el Kebir, killing some 2,000 Egyptians.

In 1883, Wolseley returned to the region to put down the revolt led by the 'Mahdi', a leader of Sudanese jihadist groups resisting control by the British-backed Egyptians and objecting to the Ottomans' lax version of Islam. General Gordon, whom we last met participating in the looting of the Qing Summer Palace, had been sent to Khartoum to oversee the withdrawal of Egyptian troops but had decided to remain there. At the Battle of El Teb, en route to try to save him, Wolseley's army killed 2,000 of the Mahdi's followers. They killed 2,500 more of those the British called 'Fuzzy Wuzzies' at the Battle of Tamai.[73] In 1898, the death of Gordon at the hands of the Mahdists would be avenged by Kitchener's army at the Battle of Omdurman with the deaths of at least 12,000 (and probably a lot more) Sudanese, many of them mown down by Maxim machine guns.

Cecil Rhodes and southern Africa

Other than Edward Colston's, the statue which has provoked most outraged commentary is that of Cecil Rhodes, who stands on a plinth above the entrance to Oriel College, Oxford. I will interrupt my Westminster walk to take an imaginary detour there.

Like Dilke, Rhodes was an ardent racial supremacist. In 1894 he told the Cape Colony's Parliament that 'if the

Bartle Frere and Rhodes

Whites maintain their position as the supreme race, the day may come when we shall be thankful that we have the natives in their proper place'. During the 1930s the Nazis admired him greatly, not least because he saw the Anglo-Saxons as a branch of the Germanic race. Spengler was inspired by him, Hitler thought that he was the only man who had understood what was necessary for continuing British supremacy and Goebbels described him as a 'rare force man'.[74]

Having left England aged 17 Rhodes made his first substantial financial returns importing water pumps to the diamond mines of Kimberley, incorporated into the Cape Colony. Rhodes amassed a fortune, establishing a diamond monopoly in the form of De Beers Consolidated by 1888. Like Clive, he then pursued mutually reinforcing political and business careers, becoming the main advocate for British imperial expansion to the north of the Cape Colony.

Rhodes' first attempt came as commissioner to southern Bechuanaland. Rather than allying with British liberals who wanted to help the BaTswana defend themselves from Boer aggression with a Protectorate administered with a light touch from London, Rhodes saw his interests better served by incorporating them into the Cape Colony, where he influenced parliament. He could then impose taxes on them. This would force them out of a subsistence economy by requiring them to earn wages in his mines. At the same time, by taking control of their land he could control further access to the north for both Britons and Boers.

In the same year that he established his monopoly, Rhodes' agents secured a concession to search for minerals from the Ndebele chief Lobengula. The following year, with Rhodes now the Cape Colony's Prime Minister, his British South Africa Company obtained a royal charter to sponsor the settler occupation of Mashonaland. The company then conquered the Ndebele in 1893. Meanwhile Rhodes invested the money made from diamonds around Kimberley in gold mining around Johannesburg, which lay within the Afrikaner (Boer) Transvaal republic. He became one of the Randlords — the magnates controlling the gold mines — and agitated for the overthrow of the Boer government, which, he argued, constrained their profitability.

After a failed attempt to overthrow the Boer government with the Jameson Raid of 1895, Rhodes and others' agitation in London eventually prompted the Second Boer War, from 1899–1902. The policies of confederation that Bartle Frere and Wolseley had furthered in South Africa worked to Rhodes' benefit, since dispossessed and taxed African men, their own independent authorities already conquered, would have no option but to work for the mining companies in the conquered Transvaal at suppressed wages — just as Rhodes had earlier intended for the BaTswana in the diamond mines.

Rhodes, however, was not content with the conquest of remaining African polities within the region already demarcated for confederation. With the conquest of the Mashona and Ndebele (Matabele) among other polities, his British South Africa Company had occupied what are now Zimbabwe and Zambia. With characteristic modesty, he named them Rhodesia. The Maxim machine gun, later put to such deadly use at Omdurman, was first tried out by British forces during the suppression of the Ndebele revolt against Rhodes' rule in 1896. Its inventor used eyewitness accounts of its effects in his advertising: 'We could see hundreds of n*****s mowed down like wheat before a scythe', and Wolseley rapidly adopted it for the British army.[75]

Rhodes' tenure as Prime Minister of the Cape included passage of the Glen Grey Act, one of the measures adopted

Bartle Frere and Rhodes

across the Empire that had the effect of denying the vote to Black men who would otherwise qualify under non-racial franchises, due to their successful farming of communal land reserves. The act overturned communal land holding and recognised only the enfranchisement of private landowners. It also imposed taxes which had to be paid in cash, meaning that African men were forced to leave the reserves — the diminished territories left after White farmers had taken their best land — to work for White employers. Rhodes justified these measures as part of an apparently non-racial call for 'equal rights for all civilised men', believing they would spur Africans on to become more 'civilised' through the saving of wages and the purchase of private land.

Rhodes, like other imperialists, thought that Black people might well be capable of such progress, only it would take generations to adapt (especially given the kind of wages they were paid — enough for single migrant men with rations and accommodation in compounds deducted, but not for the maintenance of families in the reserves). Their removal from communal land holding was a first step. More broadly the entitlement of white colonists to African labour, 'released' from the reserves, spread northwards as much of southern Africa was colonised. For example, a colonial officer in the British Protectorate of Nyasaland wrote to his mother in 1929: 'One chief has to bring me 200 men to work for nothing and he brings me some every day, but he has to bring me a lot more yet. The hatred on his face when I tell him he has to bring more still or I will make war on him is intense, but he's got to do it, or I'll burn all his villages and crops down.'[76]

Rhodes was 'obsessed about securing his own legacy', which is why he donated not only to the University of Cape Town, but also to his alma mater, Oriel College Oxford. He established the Rhodes Scholarship so that bright students, mainly from Britain's settler colonies, their offshoot, the USA, and their Anglo-Saxon relatives in Germany, could come together at Oxford, boosting Dilke's vision of a globe-spanning Greater Britain.[77] Although Rhodes' will stated that there should be no racial bar to recruitment, the four private schools specified for the receipt of scholarships in southern Africa were for Whites only. Black South African students have been able to take advantage of the scheme only since 1991, when Oxford dons mobilised to protest at the effective bar.

Given Rhodes' track record of self-interested dispossession and his veneer of non-racialism whilst doing all he could to exclude Africans from land and governance across southern Africa, it is not surprising that it was Black students of the formerly Whites-only University of Cape Town who launched the Rhodes Must Fall campaign in 2015. Now that it is threatened by Black Lives Matter protestors and their supporters extending the Rhodes Must Fall slogan from Cape Town to Oxford, the small Oriel College statue seems to stand for the integrity of all that is British among conservative populists. After commissioning an independent report, the college itself finally agreed that its removal is best but has retreated again in the face of the central government's opposition.[78]

One of Rhodes' most vocal defenders, the Oxford theologian Nigel Biggar, has stated that 'Rhodes was an imperialist, but British colonialism was not essentially racist, wasn't essentially exploitative, and wasn't essentially atrocious. So the fact that Rhodes was a supporter of the British Empire as a modernising force for good doesn't damn him'.[79] Biggar may mean that Rhodes himself did not see racism and exploitation as necessary properties in defining British colonialism, and thought of the empire, 'essentially',

Bartle Frere and Rhodes

as a force for good. This may be true, but Rhodes thought that 'good' would only be achieved by violent conquest, the denial of sovereignty and the subordination of Black people's labour to White commercial interests such as his own. When he had the opportunity to back the Bechuanaland Protectorate that created Botswana as a functioning, African-governed state, able to pick and choose which aspects of British culture to absorb, he preferred conquest and subordination within the Cape Colony for southern Bechuanaland.

Black men, who lacked civilisation as Rhodes saw it, would eventually become 'civilised' only with the help of Maxim guns, dynamite and White rule. Then, they could be subjected to superior White Anglo-Saxon influence, especially once they were taken on as cheap labour by the White settlers who had usurped their land. Even one of Rhodes' many hagiographers wrote that Rhodes was 'an advocate of educating [Africans] up to, but not beyond, their probable needs. He regarded them as grown-up children with the passions of men, and felt towards them as if, in some way, he stood in loco parentis'. As the South African historian Paul Maylam put it, this is an attitude 'that now smacks of the most awful arrogance and chauvinism'. Writing in 2005, Maylam continued, 'but for imperialists in the age of empire', it was an attitude 'that reflected noble idealism'.[80] He was not to know that Biggar and his culture warrior allies would reclaim precisely that attitude in 2020.

Retain and Explain

Returning to Westminster's crop of petrified imperial men, for all Frere's antislavery credentials, it is indisputable that both he and Wolseley's careers, as well as Rhodes', depended on Black lives mattering little compared to White lives. The main purpose of Wolseley's career was the subjugation of independent Black societies to serve British interests. The argument that these were men of their times rings true, even though these men were directly responsible for much more killing than most of their contemporaries and there were always British critics of the brutality that they dispensed against people of colour.

However, it is precisely a clear-eyed awareness of what those times were and how we might wish to mark those who contributed to them that is needed today. Defending the nostalgic, romanticised, self-congratulatory and often patently false image of the past embodied in the statues of the late nineteenth and early twentieth century not only elides the opposition of many Britons to the discriminatory and rapacious actions of their compatriots; it is also no way to ensure the wealth and well-being of a diverse British society in the future. It is quite something when a conservative military historian can still be taken seriously writing 'it is simply not true that violence was the primary feature of colonialism. Sure, there were often wars at the start, in order to secure territory (though this actually occurred far less than might be thought: the British Empire was spurred on by the desire for trade, not territory per se).'[81] This, after all that historians have written and taught about the violence intrinsic to the careers of men like Wolseley, Bartle Frere and Rhodes, and when we know that over sixty of Callwell's 'small' imperial wars were launched in the late nineteenth century alone. We seem far more capable of spotting the indoctrination achieved by pro-invasion propaganda when it comes from Putin's Russia than we are of recognising it in our own history.

My own feeling is that some statues associated with this racialised violence could be removed to museums where they can be properly contextualised, as Colston's now is.

Bartle Frere and Rhodes

Britons have learned far more British history because of its removal than they did from its standing mutely on its pedestal for over a hundred years. But I think there is also potential, depending on the circumstances of each location, to use imperial statues for the educational purposes that culture warriors falsely claim they have always had. The government's Retain and Explain policy provides opportunities here, although perhaps not of the kind Oliver Dowden anticipated when setting it out. Wherever site constraints allow, we should use statues as focal points for educating Britons about these imperial men's violent connections with peoples and places that are distanced and disavowed in the culture warriors' racially blinkered 'national story'. Imperial nostalgia works by distancing White Britons from the effects of British colonialism overseas. Let us use these statues to bridge across that distance.

Many local authorities now see the intensification of controversy over statues as an opportunity to educate Britons more about the diverse and complex history of the British Empire. Attempts at explanation of Colston's statue were successfully blocked until it was torn down, so we must ensure that a full and truthful explanation is allowed, whilst at the same time acknowledging why the statues were put up in the first place and engaging in good faith with those who are emotionally invested in them. In theory this should be allowed by the policy of Retain and Explain announced by Robert Jenrick to prevent further statue removals.

Wolseley's and Frere's statues, if interpreted with visually arresting display boards, perhaps with QR codes linking to websites for fuller context, could enable us, for instance, to consider Britain's role in the Indian Uprising and Opium Wars; the plunder of Asante treasures and the debate over their repatriation from British museums. We could further include Confederation's role in killing tens of thousands of people trying to defend their land and autonomy while creating the geographical template for apartheid in South Africa, as well as the story of early Egyptian nationalist resistance.

This will not be easy, however. When Exeter City Council announced a consultation on moving the statue of Sir Redvers Buller, one of the Wolseley 'gang' who served with him in the Red River Expedition, the Asante campaign, Southern Africa, Egypt and Sudan, it received 5,000 racially abusive emails in one day, many of them targeting councillors of colour. The council's initial decision to move Buller was reversed in the light of the central government Retain and Explain policy.

Now that this is the official policy, a difficult issue for those engaged in statue reinterpretation — the 'explain' bit of the government's mantra — is how to do this work without inflaming the racism within our communities, whilst still attending to the calls for action by those directly affected by statues and what they represent. We must strive for dialogue and negotiation if we are to seize what opportunities are available to us in the Retain and Explain policy. However, we also wonder what kind of explanation will be tolerated by the central government? Will we simply see a repeat of the saga that led to Edward Colston's toppling, where attempts to reveal truths about colonial violence are blocked in favour of yet more denial and disavowal?

The omens are not good. It is becoming evident that the 'explain' element of the central government strategy may be mere rhetoric. What is really intended by the current government's populist culture warriors seems simply to be 'retain'. In May 2021 the government set up a Heritage Advisory Board to advise on implementing Retain and

Bartle Frere and Rhodes

Explain at the national level. It comprises Museum of the Home's Samir Shah as well as Sir Trevor Phillips, and Robert Tombs, a pro-Brexit historian of Britain and France with whom I have debated the empire's racial violence.[82] Its brief is promising and Dowden said all the right things to placate concern when he announced its formation: 'History is a dynamic, living subject, and it's right that we constantly reassess and reinterpret events as our understanding evolves ... any account of the past should start from a commitment to telling a balanced, nuanced and academically rigorous story'.[83] Dowden is quite correct that the approach should be one 'that doesn't automatically start from a position of guilt and shame or the denigration of this country's past.' Neither, however, should it be one that takes patriotism and national pride as its starting point.

I am not encouraged by the terms in which Sir John Hayes, the chairman of the Common Sense group of Conservative MPs whose views we will examine in the next chapter, has endorsed the new board: 'Some of what we have heard from public bodies [about including information on slavery and colonialism] has been mischievous, some of it has been sinister and some of it has just been daft. It needs to be stopped in its tracks.' Neither is Dowden's earlier statement of intent — that we must 'must defend our culture and history from the noisy minority of activists constantly trying to do Britain down' — an auspicious start for a body supposedly pursuing a 'balanced, nuanced and academically rigorous story'. Robert Tombs has already been outspoken against the 'woke', warning that he is on the case, trying to ensure that local authorities do not pander to them, or in other words, reveal the true racial

Deny & Disavow

violence of empire, in their 'explanations'. Strikingly, there is not one historian with any expertise in British colonialism or empire on the commission.

Part Two

Chapter Four

Empire in the Culture War

The Culture War in Parliament

Our tour of some of the statues in Westminster has given us a glimpse of the British Empire's foundations in violent conquest and racial subordination, which I will elaborate upon in Part Two. Let us turn now to the image of the Empire that today's populist culture warriors are intent upon perpetuating.

Common Sense?

Almost exactly a year after Colston's toppling, around 50 Brexiteering Tory MPs styling themselves the Common Sense Group published their manifesto, 'Common Sense: Conservative Thinking for a Post-liberal Age'. It outlined their reaction to Black Lives Matter.[84] These MPs are some of the most vociferous agitators for a culture war, which they claim was started under Tony Blair's premiership when leftists encroached on conservative cultural assumptions.

'The Battle for Britain has begun', writes the group's chair, Sir John Hayes, and 'it must be won by those who, inspired by the people's will, stand for the common good in the national interest.'[85] This group's collective vision is, in places, startlingly extreme. It wants to discard Britain's uncodified liberal constitution. 'Leaving the EU', Hayes warns, 'is just the end of the beginning, not the beginning of the end of this process. What is required is nothing less than a complete reconfiguration of the relationship between the individual, society, the economy and the state.' Winning the culture war 'is vital to such a national rebirth' (a phrase often used by twentieth century fascists).

One contributor, Alexander Stafford MP, insists that their agenda 'will require both Government action and courage', most immediately: to undermine the 2010 Equality Act, repeal hate speech laws, and break up the BBC. They want to 'end the need for impartiality' in news reporting, allowing right wing news channels to disseminate anti-liberal polemic without even an attempt at objectivity. These critics of Black Lives Matter claim that the movement's demands are radically destabilising of British society. To me, they seem far less so than their own demands.

The Red Wall

During the summer of 2020, the government was on the back foot for its mishandling of the Covid 19 crisis. It had locked down too late and allowed infection rates and deaths to spiral. Boris Johnson's boast of 'world beating' track and trace systems was risible, and the early backing of vaccine development had yet to bear fruit. When the protestors pulled down Colston's statute, not only the Common Sense group of MPs but also Johnson and his cabinet, saw an opportunity to re-energise and re-mobilise the Brexit base that had yielded a large Conservative majority in the House of Commons. This majority was secured in the 2019 General Election by capturing long-held Labour seats in northern England — the so-called Red Wall. Most of the electorate there had voted strongly for Brexit and backed the

Conservative party's mantra of 'get Brexit done', regardless of any long-term cost (a cost which turns out to have been roughly 4 per cent of GDP per year).[86]

Munira Mirza among others appreciated that more permanent advantage might be gained if anti-racist activists could be banded together with other perceived cultural threats and labelled as 'woke' challenges to the conservative social attitudes of northern voters. The Johnson government's culture war entered a new phase. As Tory Brexiteers saw it, the 'Red Wall' had voted with two main agendas in mind. The first was against metropolitan liberal elites who were delaying Brexit and pandering to the 'woke'. The second was for a promised tranche of major infrastructural investment described by Johnson as 'levelling up'. The question for Johnson and the Brexiteers was how to retain their support with Brexit done, and with the shrunken post-Covid economy — its recovery hampered by Brexit induced barriers to trade and labour supply — limiting the government's ability to deliver any real 'levelling up'.

Stafford's chapter in the Common Sense group manifesto is called 'Social Conservatism — Turning the Red Wall Blue for Years to Come'. He wrote, 'We, as the Common Sense Group, believe that the Conservative Party has the opportunity to adopt a political philosophy which will keep the North and the Midlands blue for decades to come. A blue tide swept across the former "Red Wall" in December 2019, fuelled by a desire for traditional British values, for economic renewal, and for an end to the out-of-touch North London and Brussels liberal elites running our country at the expense of the population'. Ten of the MPs contributing to the Common Sense manifesto were elected for the first time in 2019 and three won traditionally non-Conservative seats.

Empire in the Culture War

Without being able to deliver economically, especially after the disastrous Liz Truss and Kwasi Kwarteng 'mini-budget' in 2022, a culture war against the 'woke' spectre became not merely a defence of values that these MPs cherish; it is also all that's left of a strategy to retain the new Tory majority.

Continued Tory momentum depended upon the creation of a new enemy — a spectre as contemptible as that of the EU conjured up before the 2016 referendum. 'Once the Brexit transition period is over', wrote Stafford, 'the Conservative Party will be at a crossroads. We must double down on the social conservatism that voters in our constituencies expect of us. We must avoid losing our way'. Conservative hyper-nationalists made a start in sketching out the new 'woke' spectre in the immediate aftermath of the Black Lives Matter protests, opening two main fronts: against the practice and teaching of Britain's colonial history and against Black Lives Matter itself.

The Common Sense group's manifesto assaults history in all its guises: academic research on the past, heritage preservation and interpretation, and teaching in schools and universities. All publicly funded practitioners, its authors believe, 'should be required to promote British values, traditions and history'. But only of a certain racially divisive kind. 'Britain is under attack', writes Gareth Bacon MP. 'Not in a physical sense, but in a philosophical, ideological and historical sense. Our heritage is under a direct assault — the very sense of what it is to be British has been called into question, institutions have been undermined, the reputation of key figures in our country's history have been traduced'. Bacon's visceral sense of endangerment reminds us that the attempted culture war is not solely about appealing to the perceived socially conservative views of red wall voters. As with conservatives in the USA, 'At bottom', as Peter Mitchell writes, 'there is the sense of betrayal and the anxiety of replacement: generational, cultural, gendered and racial. This terror is at the core of a frighteningly intense emotional charge: a sense, never quite articulated but always present, that the stakes are personal and existential.'[87]

Emotional Attachments

The Common Sense group's engagement with history reveals genuine perplexity. The story of Britishness that defined their sense of national belonging is the same as that which shaped me growing up as a White boy from a working/lower middle-class background in North London in the 1970s and 80s. I understand it. It is one of exploration, discovery, conquest, colonisation and above all, power. These are the things that I read about Britons overseas in comics and books and watched on TV. The sense of Britishness that I learned as our family moved out of a Harringay attracting ever more Cypriot and Black people in 1970, and to an Enfield that was also becoming more diverse, if a little more slowly, played out in two main theatres of White British endeavour — the Second World War and Empire.

Sometimes the Empire was portrayed in the guise of self-deprecation with films like *Carry on up the Khyber* (1968) and *The Meaning of Life* (1983) mocking Victorian notions of gallantry in the face of hordes of Black and Brown 'savages'. At other times it was more serious. The film that had the greatest impact on me was *Zulu* (1964), which acknowledged the bravery of the Zulu warriors who sought to repel Britain's invasion of Zululand in 1879. For years the film shaped my view that the Empire was essentially a contest in which 'we' had come out top, and 'they' had come to appreciate 'our' rule. But now 'they' were arriving here

Empire in the Culture War

in ever greater numbers 'they' were coming to constitute some ill-defined threat. 'They' had effectively polluted the Harringay of my early childhood.

My and others' appreciation of Britishness and its foundation in Empire was one founded on the Victorian idea of White Britons ruling over people of colour who might be British subjects, but who should remain in place, out there in the colonies where they could be safely controlled and gradually improved. It was at the same time one of White Britons civilising, Christianising and freeing those people of colour around the world who were less privileged than 'us'. There is a very strong humanitarian tradition of Empire that I have since researched extensively, which criticised the brutality of colonial rule and thought that it could be done better, but thought that it should not be done at all vanishingly rarely.

In this appreciation, the founders of the modern British nation who fought only to benefit others were White. Britain's heritage is that of a White nation only recently inundated with people of colour, many of whom seem ungrateful for the benefits that our Empire bestowed upon them. It is a version of history that denies Black people's belonging, either in Britain itself, or in 'our' national story other than as passive recipients of White British benevolence.

It did not occur to me until I was quite a bit older than when I was first gripped by the heroics portrayed in the film, *Zulu*, to read some professional historians' work so that I could understand why there were British troops in Zululand in 1879. It was that reading that led me to appreciate how their presence in Southern Africa was as much a part of British history as it was of South Africa's. In the story of Empire that shaped me and so many White Britons of my generation, the hundreds of millions of people of colour

Deny & Disavow

who were made British subjects around the world, often through unprovoked wars of conquest, could never become proper Britons themselves. Family stories of conquering, ruling and civilising were part of our history, but not those of being conquered, colonised, enslaved or exploited. Ours was a myopic, island-centred view of a vast and disparate Empire — one full of British subjects who were not British.

'Our' most rousing national anthem, even though it might not be the official one, *Rule Britannia*, declares that 'Britons never … shall be slaves'. This is not quite true though. The acts of people like Colston, enslaving African people and putting them to work on British colonial plantations, and of the 24th Regiment of Foot repelling Zulus from Rorke's Drift and helping to resume the invasion of Zululand, rendered enslaved and colonised people British subjects whether they liked it or not. So Britons, overwhelmingly the Black ones, could be both enslaved and colonised. New British subjects of colour were generated relentlessly overseas as the Empire expanded in the Americas and India, in Australasia, the Pacific and the Indian Oceans, and in Africa and the Middle East between the late seventeenth and twentieth centuries. Yet throughout it all, Britons at home imagined themselves a White nation.

The fact that most of us today still see the White colonists as British and the Black colonised as something other, something distant, something foreign, means that the descendants of today's Black British citizens are still written out of 'our' national story. Their shared Britishness is disavowed. As David Olusoga notes, 'we've created a moral firewall between what happened in Britain and what happened in the empire — with the idea that what happened in the empire doesn't really count.'[88] We all know how the slavery of the US Deep South has shaped the character

Empire in the Culture War

of America, but few of us appreciate how much Britain was shaped by its own 'Deep South' across the oceans in the Caribbean and other sites of plantation agriculture around the empire. For populist culture warriors, seeking desperately to retain that 'firewall', Britishness tends still to connote Whiteness, perhaps with the inclusion of people of colour who are sufficiently grateful.

We need, however, to start seeing slavery and the successive forms of colonialism that accompanied and followed it, as something that Britons did to other Britons, millions of descendants of whom are now living within the British Isles, if we are to move towards racial reconciliation in this country. What we have at present is like a family history that leaves out the part where one branch of the family kills another branch en masse and enslaves and exploits the survivors. Restoring this branch of the family to the family tree is not 'censoring' the past or 'undermining history'; it is completing it.

This will entail more than just an acknowledgement that Black people became British as a result of Empire — that 'they are here because we were there'. It will also entail some honesty about the way that race fundamentally configured the running of the empire. The Common Sense Group's Gareth Bacon MP most sincerely wants to believe that the British Empire was 'a modernising, civilising force that spread trade, wealth and the rule of law around the globe'. He is no doubt genuinely disoriented to be told that yes, it spread trade — but only that which was favourable to White Britons and some relatively wealthy (mainly Indian) allies, some of whose descendants still proclaim the benefits of Empire to the colonised as a whole. As we have already glimpsed from Wolseley's activities in China, free trade in British manufacturers' and merchants' interests was often

Deny & Disavow

enforced at the point of a gun. At the very same time that Manchester saw a monster anti-Corn Law demonstration to open up trade in basic staples on behalf of the British poor, British steamships and marines were forcing the Qing empire to accept an illegal trade in opium, grown for Britons by their poorer Indian subjects.

And yes, the Empire spread wealth — mainly to White Britons who either stayed at home, perhaps as absentee slave owners, or East India Company shareholders, or who emigrated to become settler landowners enjoying the services of subordinated Black labourers and servants. British settlers' wealth came from the dispossession of indigenous peoples and the violent destruction of their societies in North America, Southern Africa and Australasia. And yes, the Empire spread the rule of law — applied almost universally to maintain White supremacy, within legislative systems from which British subjects of colour were generally excluded.

The Common Sense group and their allies may choose to examine the Empire with blinkers on, or more often simply look the other way, but, as I will show in greater detail in Part Two, Britain's Empire rested, by the mid-nineteenth century, on three main geographical pillars: a tropical plantation system beginning with enslaved African labour in the Caribbean and spreading to the Pacific and Indian Oceans with the use of indentured Asian workers; the extraction of rent for Company shareholders from Indians, and their coerced production of opium to smuggle into China; and a White British diaspora of some twenty million over the course of the century, to create the settler colonies, later dominions in North America, Australasia and Southern Africa. Each of these pillars in turn rested on the subjugation of most local people of colour to serve

Empire in the Culture War

White British colonial interests, sometimes but by no means universally, with the collaboration of subordinated indigenous elites and allies such as the Indians who helped to govern and police East Africans.

The fact that both historians and activists have finally brought a sense of self and nation premised on White superiority into question, is deeply unsettling for those who have invested their identities in it. Even though the Common Sense group do not consider themselves racist, the recovery of colonised Black British subjects' experiences of the past is causing genuine bafflement among them. They feel that their virtue and their value is at stake. Having been raised on the same diet of imperial propaganda, I felt the same when I first began to read more about the reasons why British redcoats were in Zululand, and to appreciate the scale of the violence that they inflicted on the people of the region as they built the basis for a racially segregated state. However, I learned to make a distinction between personal culpability and awareness. It seems that the members of the Common Sense Group cannot bring themselves to welcome a long overdue revision of Britain's accepted national story. Instead, railing against the 'diminution of our country's stature and history,' they are seeking to preserve a racist idea of what the UK is and what it should be.

Race

The Common Sense MPs admit that 'claims of perceived injustice stem, somewhere down the line, from real injustice. Slavery was, and is, inhumane, as were the Jim Crow laws and segregation'. However, 'the ensuing Civil Rights movement was a tremendous achievement in righting those wrongs ... once those very real laws were abolished, there was left a vacuum which needed to be filled with more things to fix. As a result, although racism certainly does still exist, the real racism expanded to encompass perceived racism too'. The implications are first, that institutional racism was an American phenomenon and nothing to do with the UK, and secondly that racial inequity in the UK is now more perceived than real.

Office for National Statistics figures reveal something more troubling. Black households are the most likely out of all ethnic groups to have a weekly income of less than £400. People in White British households are consistently the least likely to live in low-income households. Across the NHS workforce in 2018, Black men were paid 84p for every £1 received by White men, and Black women 93p. When comparing staff in similar roles, White staff had higher average pay than those in all other ethnic groups. Among juveniles sentenced in 2017, the Black ethnic group had the highest percentage of offenders sent to a Young Offenders Institution. In every year during the same period, White offenders were given the shortest custodial sentences on average, and Asian or Black offenders were given the longest, for the same offences. In every socio-economic group and age group, White British households were more likely to own their own homes than all ethnic minority households combined. Despite supposed 'red wall' grievances, in every region in England and in Scotland, unemployment rates are lower for White people than for all other ethnic groups combined, with the biggest differences in West Midlands, the North-East and Yorkshire and the Humber.[89]

Despite these facts, the Common Sense group decries 'the intolerant woke dogma of Black Lives Matter', labelling it an 'extreme cultural and political group ... fuelled by ignorance and an arrogant determination to erase the past and dictate the future'. Rather than seeking to address injustices of the kind indicated by the ONS statistics, it is apparently 'motivated by darker emotions: hatred, jealously, malice, insecurity'. Behind the 'universally accepted idea that racism is wrong', the Common Sense group alleges, BLM activists 'hide other more controversial ideas such as the desirability of the destruction of the conventional family unit, smashing capitalism, defunding the police and an unpleasant strain of anti-Semitism.'

These allegations come from a highly selective reading of mainly US Black Lives Matter activists' rhetoric. There, a gun pathology associated with the right to bear arms, along with the deep schisms of race, have created the conditions in which decentralised police forces kill over a thousand people every year, a disproportionate number of them African American. Even there, however, the Black Lives Matter's demand to 'defund the police' does not mean cutting off all police funding. The argument is that 5 per cent less funding for police could be used to provide a significant boost in funding for education, healthcare and housing for poorer Black communities. This more prophylactic approach, it is hoped, might help to reduce the problems that the police have to deal with.

In the UK, the deployment of the 'defund the police' phrase has opened even greater room for misinterpretation, and I do not think it is a particularly useful or accurate way of stating the demands of most of those who support Black Lives Matter as a movement. Here too, activists want to see the redistribution of budgets rather than starving the police of funds. The official website of Black Lives Matter in the UK explains that 'Black Britons make up 12% of adult prisoners and more than 20% of children in custody — compared to just 3% of the general population'. It calls not for an end to policing, 'but instead investing in social policies that prevent people from experiencing violence and harm in the first place'. I could not find anything on the official UK Black Lives Matter website even remotely close to the idea of undermining the nuclear family unit, while anti-capitalist and pro-Palestinian views that might or might not be anti-Semitic have no doubt been expressed by many activists, but they do not seem to be part of any recognised Black Lives Matter programme.[90] The one aim that its sympathisers seem to have in common is to challenge entrenched racism and its effects.

The reality of what Black Lives Matter is, however, how it came about, what it seeks to achieve and how it defines itself, does not matter to the Common Sense group. What matters is that voters can be persuaded that its 'woke' warriors …, advocates of 'decolonisation' and 'White privilege' are 'destroying the fabric of British society'. Apparently without irony, the same contributor goes on to note that 'A country divided into rigid identity groups which refuse to accept the validity of differing points of view would soon become ungovernable'.

The Conservative Party's commitment to culture war has been uneven, waxing and waning according to especially volatile political contingencies since the Common Sense group published their manifesto. To a certain extent, the focus of key proponents like Suella Braverman and Kemi Badenoch has shifted from empire and race to transgender people's rights, represented as an assault on women and biological 'common sense'. Any further exposition of Britain's colonial history still acts as a trigger for many of those on the right though. When he was contesting the party leadership with Liz Truss in 2022, Rishi Sunak declared that he was not interested in culture war. He immediately

Empire in the Culture War

contradicted himself by assuring his audience that he would 'safeguard our shared cultural, historical and philosophical heritage' against 'left-wing agitators' who supposedly want 'to take a bulldozer to our history, our traditions and our fundamental values'. Sounding very much like the populist Johnson whom he had helped to unseat, Sunak vowed to resist 'pulling down statues of historic figures, replacing the school curriculum with anti-British propaganda, or rewriting the English language so we can't even use words like "man", "woman" or "mother" without being told we're offending someone'. Meanwhile, Braverman, his reinstated anti-immigrant Home Secretary who seeks the support of Common Sense's Hayes, insists that she is 'proud of the British Empire' as a key part of her populist platform.[91]

Chapter Five

The Race Report

In the wake of the toppling of Colston's statue, Boris Johnson promised the appointment of a commission to report, definitively, on issues of racial inequity. Munira Mirza led the selection of its members. Commissions are generally appointed by governments in search of independent, evidence-based findings. They are supposed to strive for objectivity and their findings are the result of investigation rather than executive instruction. However, Johnson seems uncannily to have anticipated this commission's narrative, even as it was announced. 'I think this is a country that has made huge progress in tackling racism', he declared. 'We should look sometimes at the positive stuff — we've got more young Black and minority ethnic kids going to university than ever before, more Black kids doing the tougher subjects at school, doing better than ever before in school. We don't hear enough of this positive stuff.'[92]

Mirza advised that the Brixton-raised Black educator Tony Sewell be appointed Chair and that other commissioners of colour with notable achievements be recruited. This would be a commission comprised of racial minorities stating that allegations of racism against their own communities were outdated and overblown. Sewell had already declared that the 'evidence for institutional racism is somewhat flimsy'.[93] They reported in March 2021.[94] The Report of the

The Race Report

Commission on Race and Ethnic Disparities is perhaps most powerful weapon in the government's culture war arsenal.

As subsequent policy pronouncements and reports based upon the commission's report indicate, it is a bedrock of the government's denial and disavowal strategy against Black Lives Matter. The report fleshes out, suspiciously neatly, the narrative that Boris Johnson first drafted in June 2020. The authors are very clear that 'We have argued against bringing down statues'.[95]

Sewell's Report seeks to establish a clear break between past and present, and it blames certain Black people themselves for their experiences of marginalisation and exclusion. 'For some groups historic experience of racism still haunts the present', it declares. Those of Caribbean descent are particularly to blame for their failure to appreciate that 'the system is [no longer] deliberately rigged against ethnic minorities'. By contrast, 'it is counterproductive and divisive' to suggest that 'White people's attitudes and behaviours ... primarily cause the disadvantage experienced by ethnic minorities'. Indeed, Britain is a shining beacon, a model of racial equality for other countries to follow.

Understanding History

When it comes to teaching British history, the Report identifies very clearly what it is for and what it is against. It is for a 'Making of Modern Britain' teaching resource, which shows how 'Britishness influenced the Commonwealth and local communities, and how the Commonwealth and local communities influenced ... modern Britain'. 'One great example', it continues, 'would be a dictionary or lexicon of well-known British words which are Indian in origin'. Such a resource would presumably enlighten British students about the origin of words such as 'shampoo' and 'bungalow'. It might be a bit more suspect about including the word 'loot', however, just in case a greater knowledge of colonial plunder generates further pressure on British museums to repatriate objects taken in campaigns of conquest and Britain's 'small wars'.

Presumably, this resource would also avoid any consideration of how the empire, which became the Commonwealth, was governed. It wasn't just Macaulay who felt that Indians were unfit for a share in that governance when he explained the rationale for East India Company rule in 1833. In the late 1870s, when the administration of India was centred in the government's India Office, the British architect of the Indian Penal Code, James Fitzjames Stephen noted that 'If the ... delusion that (Govt) can be carried out by ... the natives is admitted, nothing but anarchy and ruin can ... result'. This too, I suspect, might be omitted from the kind of teaching resource advocated by the commission.[96]

Promisingly, the Report is for a 'teaching resource that looks at the influence of the UK, particularly during the Empire period'. However, the initial example of the content that might be provided was disappointing to say the least: 'There is a new story about the Caribbean experience which speaks to the slave period not only being about profit and suffering but how culturally African people transformed themselves into a re-modelled African/Britain.' This would not be a new story at all. British slave traders and owners told a similar story when they sought to resist abolition and emancipation in the late eighteenth and early nineteenth centuries: Africans could only ever be culturally transformed and improved, they claimed, if they were extracted from the mire of savagery in which they were sunk in Africa

The Race Report

and exposed to the better example of British owners on Caribbean plantations.[97]

Unusually, the commission issued an addendum to try to deflect the widespread criticism of this suggestion, arguing that its intent had been to emphasise cultural resilience in the face of slavery. Nevertheless, if slavery is to be taught in this new resource, all the indications are that arguments like those of the Rhodes defender, Nigel Biggar CBE, would be propagated. In a briefing intended for politicians, Biggar suggests that Britain absolved itself of the crime of slavery when it abolished the institution in some of its colonies in 1833 (the same year that Macaulay justified the governance of Indians by British shareholders). Thereafter, the British Empire was, according to Biggar, characterised mainly by antislavery activity. As we have seen from Bartle Frere's career as anti-slavery activist turned violent conqueror of African peoples, things were a bit more complicated. I will outline the rather different consensus among historians who specialise in the British Empire in Part Two.

Creating Britishness

The Report seems to be for teaching a grand pretence: that the British Empire was a way of encouraging people of colour around the world to feel included in Britishness. 'We want all children to reclaim their British heritage', the authors claim, making it seem as if that British heritage was something voluntarily acquired by Black Britons' ancestors. In effect it says: let's pretend that the British Empire peacefully extended the benefits of Britishness to people of colour. Never mind all that unpleasantness. The violent conquest of people of colour by men like Clive, Wolseley, Bartle Frere and Rhodes, entailed in acquiring and keeping colonies, it seems, will not be featuring in this Report's proposed teaching resource. The reality that even after initial conquest, the Empire's everyday administration was conditioned by racist assumptions and the threat of violence seems even less likely to feature.[98]

The government's Race Report's refusal to acknowledge that the British Empire was not only founded on, but also governed according to such racial division fuels further division today rather than healing it.

Decolonising

The Race Report is decidedly against 'calls for decolonising the curriculum' because these are apparently 'negative'. They involve merely 'the banning of white authors or token expressions of black achievement'. This is a gratuitous misrepresentation of decolonisation, as egregious as the ones we hear repeatedly of Black Lives Matter's goals. Those who call for a project of decolonisation are not advocating any such restrictive or tokenistic agenda. They wish, rather, to extend students' knowledge beyond White authors (something that the Report itself gestures somewhat clumsily towards when it recommends 'writers in the Commonwealth, such as Derek Walcott, Seamus Heaney [an Irish author subsequently removed in another corrective amendment], and Andrea Levy'), to understand the ways that people of colour were made British subjects, and to challenge ways of thinking about difference and the 'knowledge' that we have inherited from colonialism. Let us hope that the Report's envisaged 'credible, high-quality, online national library ... enhancing the content and quality of lessons taught' includes something of the truth of the British Empire, rather than the blinkered,

The Race Report

self-congratulatory and nostalgic vision propagated by culture warriors like those in the Common Sense group. 'Understanding different perspectives and contested events is', the authors acknowledge, 'central to the study of history and should help to equip pupils to navigate a world of "fake news" and clashing opinions and truths.' Indeed. For as Sathnam Sanghera has noted, 'Our collective amnesia about the fact that we were, as a nation, wilfully white supremacist and occasionally genocidal, and our failure to understand how this informs modern day racism, are catastrophic.'[99]

Since the report was published, experts across the board, including those who were apparently consulted by it, have objected to its methods, sources and interpretation of data.[100] It is standard practice for the reports of government commissions to be reviewed in whole, draft form, by independent experts, before publication. This does not seem to have happened with the Race Report. In a Channel 4 podcast, Sewell admitted that each section author got a peer review from sources of their own and that there was no overall, independent peer review of the report. Later, he added that Eric Kauffman, a political scientist known for his anti-'wokeness' reviewed the whole thing, but it is not clear whether this was prior to publication.[101] Sewell also mentioned John Pullinger, from the UK statistics authority, as a reviewer, but Pullinger said he did not really peer review. He was given the draft a day before publication and asked what he thought about the data.[102]

The Runnymede Trust noted the cherry-picking of data on school attainment thresholds. In stating that 'Chinese, Indian, Mixed White/other and White Irish have better attainment thresholds [than White children] across ... four age groups', the report implies that White pupils are disadvantaged. What the selection of these four age groups elides is that, 'for ages 4–5, 10–11, 16 year olds at GCSE and 18 year olds at A-level, mixed White/Black African, White other, Pakistani, Black other, mixed White/Black Caribbean, Black Caribbean, Irish traveller and Gypsy/Roma all have lower attainment rates … compared to their White counterparts'. This is part of a consistent pattern in which the report uses rhetoric which pits the White working class against ethnic minorities, suggesting that for the White working class the 'door may be only half open'. However, even when White working-class boys have lower educational attainment, they have substantially higher rates of employment and social mobility than Black boys, something that the Report also neglects to mention.[103] The effect of this cherry picking of data is to fit the positive narrative that Johnson outlined before Mirza even convened the commission.

A key part of the problem that experts have with the report is the commissioners' thinking on what racial disparity means. Jonathan Portes, Professor of Economics and Public Policy at King's College London, and contributor to previous, rather more credible, government reports, points to perhaps its greatest flaw. Its methodology, he notes, 'excluded the possibility of finding that differences in outcomes are the result of race' from the very beginning. First, 'it divides observed disparities into two categories: "explained" and "unexplained".'

To extract from Portes: 'Explained racial disparities: this term should be used when there are persistent ethnic differential outcomes that can demonstrably be shown to be as a result of other factors such as geography, class or sex.

'Unexplained racial disparities: persistent differential outcomes for ethnic groups with no conclusive evidence about the causes. This applies to situations where a disparate

The Race Report

outcome is identified, but there is no evidence as to what is causing it.

'So, disparities are either explained by factors other than racism — or there is insufficient evidence, so they are unexplained. Thus, apparently, while racism does exist (and the Commission goes on to set out its own definitions of systemic, structural and institutional racism), there is no way, within its framework, to demonstrate, through the use of evidence or analysis, that racism or discrimination, indirect or direct, is actually causing the observed disparities in outcomes. Therefore, it is not that the Commission did not find any evidence that disparities are the result of race or racism — it excluded the possibility *ex ante* ... It is hard to find something if it is not being looked for. And it's even harder to do so if a methodology is used which excludes, by definition, even the possibility of finding it.'[104]

Commissioned reports are supposed to result in evidence-based policy making. But as Portes points out, 'The report is better viewed as "rhetoric-based evidence making" ... The impact of someone's race on their health cannot be dismissed by saying "well, actually, poverty is the real cause", if poverty and race are — as they are in the UK — inextricably linked ... poverty and urbanity are not "confounding factors" when it comes to assessing the impact of race on outcomes; they are potential channels ... This does not mean that race or racism drives everything — that would be equally reductive. What it does mean is that, if racial (or other) disparities are to be understood, they have to be unpicked and what is driving what needs to be thought about. But "explaining them away" — and hence giving up on doing any serious or credible analysis — is precisely what the Commission has sought to do.'[105]

Despite the fact that 'it is almost impossible to find a

topic on which someone with acknowledged expertise has not demolished the report's analysis or complained about the distortion or misrepresentation of their own research', the report has now entered the government's armoury of 'objective data' from which to draw in waging its culture war.

Although it appears not have been properly peer reviewed before publication, it was sent in advance to Mirza's culture war allies in the press, the *Sun*, *Mail* and *Telegraph*. Not to the *Independent* or the *Guardian*. Its role as culture war ammunition clearly outweighed any benefit that may come from its actual recommendations, at least in the short term.

The report's role as ammunition in a government-sponsored culture war is obvious. It is intended to stall the further momentum in anti-racist reform that Black Lives Matter protestors urged, explicitly geared to delegitimise their grievances. Rather than seizing the opportunity of the protests in June 2020 to acknowledge the wrongs of the past and provide a more reconciliatory history, the Race Report seems intent on reassuring resistant White Britons that they need not take the trouble to understand Black Britons' experiences of racism. Racism, just as they long suspected, is all in the minds of Black people, especially those of Caribbean descent. If they are not mistaken about their own experiences, then they are deliberately 'playing the race card'.

A start was made in deploying the report's rhetoric rather than its recommendations to underpin policy in June 2021, with the publication of another report from the House of Commons Education Committee titled 'The Forgotten: How White Working-class Pupils Have Been Let Down, and How to Change it'. This second report acknowledges that 'Evidence ... highlighted that there are performance measures on which pupils from ethnic minorities,

The Race Report

particularly ... Black Caribbean pupils, perform similarly or less well than disadvantaged White pupils'. Rather than adopting an approach focused on assisting both Black and White poorer pupils in response, however, the committee chose to pick a fight with the Black Lives Matter movement based upon the 'evidence' supplied by the Race Report. 'We are concerned that the phrase ('White privilege') ... may have contributed towards a systemic neglect of White people facing hardship who also need specific support', the report declares, with absolutely no evidence that the use of this phrase by any person anywhere at any time has actually impacted educational outcomes for any White pupil.[106] It leaves one thinking that the authors care more about mobilising White grievances in the culture war than they do about assisting poorer British pupils. The contrast with footballer Marcus Rashford's campaign for free school meals for poorer pupils regardless of race could not be greater

Chapter Six

Heritage

Restore Trust

Right wing conservatives' conjoined attack on Black Lives Matter and defence of the British Empire has spilled well beyond Parliament and the government's commissioned Race Report. They have made our national heritage sector a key battleground too. Calling themselves Restore Trust, a private company that claims to represent members and former members of the National Trust for whom Charles Moore, former *Telegraph* editor and friend of Boris Johnson, acts as a spokesman, has bemoaned the National Trust's supposed surrender to 'wokeness'. This came after the National Trust commissioned a report to find out more about the role that slave trading, slave ownership and colonial activities played in its properties' history. A precedent had already been set by Stephanie Barczewski's book *Country Houses and the British Empire*, which noted that that hundreds of landed estates and country houses were funded with imperial wealth between 1700 and 1930.[107]

Many Britons still see National Trust properties and especially the stately homes of the elite as cherished symbols of Britain's illustrious past, embodying ideals of order, splendour and continuity. It is unsurprising that any public

Heritage

reassessment of their history highlighting racial exploitation is galling to some. However, extremists are now trying to turn a minority of National Trust members' potential discomfort into an insurrection within the charity. Restore Trust has twice tried to get its candidates elected to the National Trust's council to combat the charity's intention to reflect openness and diversity. Although Restore Trust has been obtuse about its funding sources, there are indications that it is part of a network of extreme conservative 'think tanks' and lobbying groups associated with the premises at 55 Tufton Street in London. One of six people in Restore Trusts' Meet the Team webpage is Neil Record, a billionaire former currency risk manager and Conservative donor who backed the Institute of Economic Affairs. This was the free market, libertarian 'think tank'/lobby group which encouraged Liz Truss's disastrous minibudget in 2022. Record also chairs the Global Warming Policy Forum, which is sceptical of human-induced climate change.[108]

In 2021, Restore Trust tried to force the resignation of the National Trust's chair, Tim Parker. Parker had already extended his tenure to see the organisation through the worst of the Covid crisis, and he resigned before they could get to him. Nevertheless they claimed victory in forcing him out. They also tried to get the National Trust in trouble with the charities regulator for acting outside its charitable purposes by commissioning the report on slavery and colonialism. Despite around 150 newspaper articles in the *Mail, Telegraph, Express* and *Spectator* against the National Trust, the Charities Commission found that it had acted in line with its charitable purposes. There were no grounds for regulatory action.[109]

In November 2022, after a more concerted and seemingly better-funded propaganda campaign, Restore Trust failed

Deny & Disavow

once again to undermine the Trust's board, with the attempted election of six favoured councillors at the AGM. One of them was Stephen Green, who was national director of the far-right lobby group Christian Voice. He has previously referred to homosexuality as a 'deviant lifestyle' and supported a bill in Uganda that would have imposed capital punishment for gay sex, as well as arguing that it is impossible for a husband to rape his wife.[110] Other Restore Trust candidates are also members of the academic network History Reclaimed, which I will come onto in the next chapter.

In a statement, the National Trust itself said: 'Restore Trust is a private company that aims to influence the National Trust's council and decision-making, and has espoused a range of misleading and inaccurate views. The National Trust works well with a range of supporter groups and critics and has done so for decades … Until now, there has been no instance of paid-for campaigns to influence the charity's decisions or get individuals onto our governing bodies. We have a long, proud tradition of openness and healthy democratic processes underpinning our governance, and this will continue.'[111]

If Moore, Record, Parker and the Restore Trust's other members are upset by the Trust offering more information to visitors, one must ask why? After all, it is not as if Trust volunteers are being trained to grip its members in a headlock when they visit a property, drag them to a new interpretation board telling them that they are all racists, and supply them with whips for obligatory self-flagellation as they read about the nefarious activities of their ancestors. Visitors are free to ignore information about the origins of owning families' wealth, just as they are to ignore the other contextual information that the Trust routinely supplies about those families' lives, the architecture, design and

Heritage

provenance of the buildings, and their furniture, paintings and textiles.

Despite the protestations of the Restore Trust group, no one's experience of visiting a property will be altered by this expanded knowledge unless their curiosity gets the better of them and they seek it out on a website or interpretation board. Yet the *Telegraph* writer, Ben Lawrence, complained that his 'straightforward enjoyment' of National Trust properties, museum and gallery exhibitions is being spoilt: 'Wouldn't you rather spend your free time marvelling at the Elizabethan splendours of Hardwick Hall in Derbyshire, not being reminded of the troubled history of the Cavendish family and their links to our colonial past ... straightforward enjoyment, it seems, is no longer an option.'[112] One has to pity the poor columnist, having his leisure time ruined by the opportunity to learn historical context. But of course, in populist discourse, it is those providing the information who are the 'snowflakes', in this culture war, not those like Lawrence who might be discomfited by reminders of an unpleasant past.

My nearest property, Sheffield Park, has beautiful gardens enjoyed by my children on many visits over the years (even if they did sometimes illicitly climb on the trees when they were younger). The National Trust website entry still tells of the eighteenth-century landscape designers Capability Brown and Humphrey Repton, of Arthur Soames who owned it in the early twentieth century, of the cricket matches that were played there, and of its use by the Canadian military during World War II. The new report takes none of this away. It adds that the park's first owner, Thomas West, 3rd Baron De La Warr (1577–1618), was the first Lord Governor of the Virginia Company of London in 1609 and that the Delaware tribe, bay and river — as well

Deny & Disavow

Sheffield Park

as the US state — are named after him. I learned from the report, available online, that in 1769, the property was sold to John Baker Holroyd (1735–1821), later the 1st Earl of Sheffield, who defended the Atlantic slave trade. He wrote that 'nothing is more vain and empty than the idea that the British Legislature could immediately abolish slavery' and denounced the 'madness' of the anti-slavery movement in a speech against the abolition of the slave trade in the House of Commons.[113]

Charles Moore alleges that the National Trust's report passes judgement rather than simply illuminating the past. This seems to me untrue. The bald statement of facts about Sheffield Park's owners passes no judgement. I pass my own judgement in learning them and my extra understanding is going to make me visit Sheffield Park more often, so that my own and my children's knowledge of history can be enhanced. I have no intention of making them feel guilty about that history.

Heritage

The distinction between awareness and guilt seems as lost on Restore Trust as it does among their Common Sense parliamentary allies. The owners of Harewood House in Yorkshire were far more invested in slavery than those of Sheffield Park, but there too, the tone of the National Trusts's new information, should anyone choose to read it, is neutral and uncontroversial. We are told, 'The story of the wealth upon which this house was built begins in the West Indies, where significant fortunes were made on the back of the transatlantic slave trade. This encompassed the systematic enslavement, transportation and exploitation of African people by European traders. It was a trade that was pervasive across British society. Based in Barbados during the early eighteenth century, Henry Lascelles sought to control every aspect of the sugar trade... and in 1738 using enormous profits from the slave trade [he] purchased the combined estates of Harewood and Gawthorpe. By the time of Henry's death in 1753, he was one of the wealthiest men in England.'[114] This hardly justifies Sir John Hayes' concern, expressed in the *Telegraph*, that 'history must be neither sanitised nor rewritten to suit 'snowflake' preoccupations. A group of powerful, privileged liberals must not be allowed to rewrite our history in their image.'[115]

Restore Trust's attacks on the National Trust have lately been cloaked in the guise of support for volunteers and curators laid off due to financial concerns during the Covid lockdowns. But there are clearly political motivations too. Around a third of the National Trust's properties were built, extended, restored or owned by people engaged in colonial activities. Enraged by this finding, Moore explains the Trust's new work on the history of its properties as a knee-jerk response to 'the murder of George Floyd ... and the ensuing propaganda pile-on to British institutions by Black Lives Matter', a movement which he describes as 'wholly, violently political, and wholly unconnected with the care of Britain's heritage'.

As Colston's toppling shows, Black Lives Matter is all about Britain's heritage. It forces us to confront the question of whether Black people belong to it — whether their ancestral history matters as much as white Britons'. The national heritage that Moore claims to defend by attempting to censor what the National Trust can say about its properties is one of colonised Black British subjects' violent dispossession, enslavement, coercion and exploitation, as much as it is one of White Britons' generation of wealth and power. The specific National Trust properties that were associated with slave owners and beneficiaries of colonial exploitation are testament to both sides of this story. The blinkers that the Restore group want us to wear when we visit these places are those of race. Thankfully, to date, the vast majority of National Trust members seem to agree that these racial blinkers on our past should be removed.

As Culture secretary, however, Oliver Dowden did agree with Moore, summoning Britain's leading heritage organisations to a meeting at which he laid down the new culture war law. Declaring that 'Heritage organisations should be free from government meddling' he proceeded to block the reappointment of a Trustee on the board of Greenwich museums because he didn't like his 'woke' views, and then announced his intention to replace 'metropolitan bubbles' on the boards of Britain's leading heritage bodies with 'Red Wall voters'. These gritty northern conservatives, he hoped, would 'stop boards bowing to pressure from 'woke' activists over contested history … giving them the courage to stand up against the political fads and noisy movements of the moment'.[116]

Heritage

Our Newspapers

Restore Trust have fierce allies in the right wing press, persistently pressing home the 'war on woke' in the heritage sector with hyperbolic articles. The torrent of hysterical reaction to small things, such as the decision in May 2021 of some Oxford graduate students to take down a picture of the Queen that their predecessors had put up in their college common room, became relentless and overwhelming after June 2020. Matthew Katzman, the American PhD student and president of the Oxford common room in question, was forced to leave the country due to the torrent of abuse and death threats that followed the press campaign against him.[117]

On just one day in June 2021, the *Mail on Sunday* fulminated that 'Britain needs a leader who stands up for common sense, who doesn't buy into this narrative that Britain is a horrible hellhole, who doesn't make the vast majority of good, ordinary people feel bad for not flagellating themselves day and night in pursuit of cultural purification', while the *Sunday Telegraph* ranted that 'the current culture war is raging because what the Far-Leftists who initiated it want to do is all but impossible. They want to "decolonise" our society, which means to strip away anything connected with a long period of British history, including our reigning monarch. They want to make all White people feel guilty and feel ashamed of their skin colour. In a White majority country'.[118]

To give just a couple of examples of heritage-based culture war stories among the many that have appeared lately: In June 2021 the *Mail Online* published a story about the English Heritage blue plaque dedicated to the children's author Enid Blyton. The substance of the story was that a website accompanying the plaque was to have added context about Blyton, explaining that her racism and xenophobia were objected to during her lifetime, and even more now. The plaque itself was untouched and no new information appeared alongside it. You had to look up the English Heritage website to read this new contextual information. Yet the *Mail*'s headline was 'Now Enid Blyton is cancelled.' The response from its online subscribers was exactly what the paper had intended. The vast majority of the roughly four thousand respondents were led to believe that the 'woke' had banned and even burned Blyton's books, that English Heritage was 'destroying the past of these islands' and that Britons were being prevented from free speech just like in North Korea and Nazi Germany.

Similarly, the *Mail*'s interpretation of Kew Gardens' decision to supply additional information on the role of slavery in the history of sugar production generated the headline 'Kew Gardens is growing woke!' and elicited comments such as 'Somebody please expose and name these people who are peddling this anti-Britain, guilt-ridden agenda' and 'I will never go to Kew Gardens again'.

Given this kind of media-generated hysteria, Britain's heritage has become politicised in sinister ways I would never have imagined just a few years ago. There is but a short step from the kind of rhetoric in the *Mail*'s online forums on heritage reinterpretation to the belief of the trans-national extreme right in The Great Replacement, or White genocide. This bizarre notion of an existential threat to 'our' racial survival stemming from fellow citizens of colour is what motivated the terrorists who committed the atrocities in Oslo in 2011 and Christchurch in 2019, and the murderer of the Labour MP Jo Cox in 2016. He saw her as a 'collaborator', undermining the indigenous White race through her support for immigrants. The same rhetoric of

Heritage

White Britons becoming a minority can be found in the responses to whichever outraged headline is generated, day in and day out, in the *Mail*'s 'war on woke'.

While it might be more subtle, the *Telegraph*'s use of 'woke' is also not so far from the idea of a 'collaborator' with the forces threatening a 'White majority country'. Boris Johnson's advisor on race, Samuel Kasumu, quit in April 2021, complaining that 'some people in the government ... feel like the right way to win is to pick a fight on the culture war and to exploit division.' These elements, Kasumu feared, were facilitating a repeat of the murder of Jo Cox'.[119]

Culture wars work by replacing thought, reflection, listening and debate with immediate, pre-cognitive, triggered, emotional reaction. Dog whistle keywords like 'cancel culture', 'no-platforming' and 'censorship' are used by the *Mail* and others to manufacture outrage based not on the story, but on what the story must be about. All this has a steady drip-feed effect injecting poison into the national lifeblood. 'Respectable' American Republicans, far from the extreme fringes of the Right, thought they could manipulate culture war to their political advantage, as do many reasonably moderate Conservative MPs today. The Republicans ended up with Donald Trump, their country disgraced and a Nazi-sympathising mob invading their legislature. 'As true conservatives once knew', Nick Cohen, writes, 'it's best to avoid picking fights when you have no idea how they will end.'[120]

Chapter Seven

Academia

Populist culture warriors in government and the press have found allies among a relatively small but vocal group of academics, who are determined to defend the reputation of the British Empire in the face of overwhelming historical evidence of its systematic racial violence.[121] In August 2021, a group of scholars including Robert Tombs of the government's new Heritage Advisory Board, Niall Ferguson, Andrew Roberts and the ubiquitous Nigel Biggar, banded together to create the History Reclaimed Project, now a private company like its ally Restore Trust. Two of the group's members, Zareer Masani and Jeremy Black, stood as Restore Trust candidates in the 2022 National Trust council elections.

Nigel Biggar appears regularly in the conservative media as a pundit on the history of empire, complaining about his and his colleagues' mainstream views being suppressed within academia.[122] 'Professor Biggar', the *Daily Mail* informs us, 'insists that the history of the British empire was "morally mixed" — some bad and some good — and has been accused of racism for failing to toe the line that the empire was uniformly evil.'[123] The criticism that academics who actually research the Empire as their specialism have levelled at Biggar and his allied academic culture warriors is, of course, not for any refusal to see the empire as 'evil'. An historian would not be taken very seriously if the extent of their analysis was to declare complex phenomena that

Academia

affected people differentially across the globe over some three hundred years, as simply 'good' or 'evil'. Analysing Empire as a 'mix' of good and evil is not much better. Even at primary school we teach history in a more sophisticated manner than that.

The criticism that Biggar and his colleagues have sustained from historians is for their refusal to acknowledge that the British imperial rule was, to an overwhelming extent, premised on racial distinctions. In May 2021, 58 of Nigel Biggar's Oxford colleagues who actually research imperialism, rather than theology — Biggar's specialism — signed a public letter declaring that his outspoken statements in the media were entirely at odds with their knowledge of British colonialism. Their letter was used as a pretext by the government to introduce a bill in the Queen's Speech against supposed 'censorship' in British universities, although no one had prevented Biggar from saying whatever he wanted, usually in more prominent mainstream media outlets than his critics. Unlike Restore Trust's intention to gag the National Trust, there had been no attempt to prevent Biggar publicising his 'findings', just a questioning of their veracity in accord with the right of free speech.

Explaining that 'We teach our students to think seriously and critically about those histories and their contemporary legacies', the authors stated explicitly that 'Professor Biggar has every right to hold and to express whatever views he chooses or finds compelling, and to conduct whatever research he chooses in the way he feels appropriate. But his views on this question, which have been widely publicised at the Oxford Union, as well as in national newspapers, risk being misconstrued as representative of Oxford scholarship. For many of us, and more importantly for our students, they also reinforce a pervasive sense that contemporary inequalities in access to and experience at our university are underpinned by a complacent, even celebratory, attitude towards its imperial past. We therefore feel obliged to express our firm rejection of them'.

The problem, these specialists reported, is that 'Biggar sets up a caricature in place of an antagonist: an allegedly prevailing orthodoxy that 'imperialism is wicked'. His project's declared aim is to uncover a more complex reality, whose 'positive aspects' dispassionate scholarship can reveal. This is nonsense. No historian ... argues simply that imperialism was 'wicked'. Good and evil may be meaningful terms of analysis for theologians. They are useless to historians ... However seriously intended, far from offering greater nuance and complexity, Biggar's approach is too polemical and simplistic to be taken seriously ... We have never believed it is sufficient to dismiss imperialism as simply 'wicked'. Nor do we believe it can or should be rehabilitated because some of it was 'good'.[124]

History Reclaimed

The History Reclaimed company, which has rallied other scholars around Biggar, introduces its project as defending a 'shared history' and speaks of British society needing 'a sense of common purpose and self-worth'. It claims that these attributes are being undermined by historians and activists who draw attention to the racialised violence of colonialism. A 'shared history', it says, 'is a necessary foundation for a successful democracy'. The language betrays the most problematic element of the way that populist culture warriors more broadly have responded to the challenge of Black Lives Matter. For the history that this group defends is far from 'shared'. It is a history created by White Britons since the high point of Empire itself to deny and disavow the subordination of racialised others.

Academia

To give just a couple of examples of topics in which History Reclaimed have been vocal, in 2022, the Horniman Museum in London agreed to return artefacts known as Benin Bronzes to Nigeria. The decision sent History Reclaimed members have into overdrive, justifying the invasion of the kingdom that led to the plunder of the items in 1897 and finding spurious grounds upon which to prevent their return. Their reaction was based on three main arguments. The first was that Benin was a slave trading state, which both legitimated the British assault and renders repatriation morally problematic. This is conveniently to forget that states like Benin were stimulated to engage in slave raiding by the demand from Europeans. The largest 'cargoes' for the Middle Passage were sold to Britons from the early eighteenth century up to 1807, by which time Benin was no longer a major slave trading state.

Their second argument was that the British 'punitive expedition' that plundered the artefacts was intended to abolish slavery in Nigeria. It was not. British traders had been lobbying officials to overthrow the Oba, as they had other leaders in what is now Nigeria, for years, without any expression of antipathy to slavery. What they objected to was the limits on their profits from palm oil and ivory that derived from having to pay tariffs to the Oba. British officials acting on the traders' behalf tried to force negotiation on ending this aspect of Benin sovereignty with a diplomatic mission, but having witnessed the British kidnapping and deposition of other rulers in the region, the Oba told them to stay away. When an official British party ignored the injunction and entered the kingdom, they were attacked and most killed.

Acting Consul James Phillips, the leader of this party, had written to the Foreign Office before his departure to say that he intended 'to depose and remove the King of Benin and to establish a native council in his place'. He reported that he had with him 'a sufficient armed Force, consisting of 250 troops, two seven pounder guns, 1 Maxim, and 1 rocket apparatus ... and a detachment of Lagos Hausas 150 strong.' He appended the postscript: 'I would add that I have reason to hope that sufficient ivory may be found in the King's house to pay the expenses in removing the king from his stool'.[125] Yet Nigel Biggar's justification for the subsequent expedition is based on the 'massacre' of this 'diplomatic mission', whose nine White members, led by Phillips, had been unarmed (apart from revolvers!).[126]

The killing of Phillips and his force provided the British traders and officials in the region with their pretext for the 1897 expedition. The rhetoric about stamping out slavery was post-invasion justification. Historians who know the region and its history, and have studied the British sources, have long pointed this out, but it suits defenders of British imperialism to believe the propaganda of the immediate post-invasion period. This also included overblown and lurid accounts by expedition members of the Oba's atrocities against enslaved people including the bodies of those supposedly killed in human sacrifices, many of whom may actually have been killed in indiscriminate rocketing and shellfire during the British assault.[127]

History Reclaimed's third justification for retaining the plunder from the assault on Benin consists of tales from the 1970s–90s of Nigerian museums being unable to prevent the theft of artefacts and the 'lesson' that the bronzes should stay 'safe' in UK museums. These suggestions directly reproduce colonial tropes that African institutions are not sophisticated enough to look after their assets. The repatriated bronzes will in reality be going to a purpose built, state of the art museum and visitor centre where both local people and tourists can view them.[128] Despite all this being known, History Reclaimed still hosts an article claiming that 'the expedition to overthrow [the Oba] found at his palace revolting atrocities which are not much mentioned these days, and the antiquities it sold to defray its cost are referred to as "loot". But this loot had saved a great many Africans from a life of slavery, or from death as one of the bloodthirsty Oba's human sacrifices'.

A further example of History Reclaimed's tendentious approach to history is another of its favourite themes — the antislavery patrols mounted by the Royal Navy in the aftermath of the British abolition of the slave trade in 1807. Contributors laud the British for being the first to abolish the trade (Denmark abolished its own trade a year beforehand), for the bravery of the naval personnel involved in capturing other nations' slave ships, and for incurring the considerable human and financial costs of the trade's suppression. Much of this is quite reasonable and has been a feature of the specialist literature on abolition all along. But what is new about History Reclaimed's approach is its conscious selectivity.[129]

Unlike scholarly accounts which strive for an holistic appreciation of Britain's antislavery activity, History Reclaimed adherents tend to neglect the strategic motivation to prevent rival nations continuing to profit from the trans-Atlantic trade when Britain had abolished its own; that in the late nineteenth century antislavery measures were a pretext for the violent conquest of African societies such as Benin, followed by racially discriminatory rule; and above all, that most of the captives freed from other nations' ships by the Royal Navy were never repatriated. Instead they were either forcibly recruited into the British military or assigned as unpaid 'apprentices' to planters and settlers (including Black Sierra Leonians) for 12-15 years. 'Runaways' were recaptured and returned to their masters and mistresses as if they were still enslaved. Finally, History Reclaimed contributors tend to claim that British actions against the slave trade of other nations is a suppressed story in these days of prevailing 'wokeness'. This is untrue. It is, rather, the fate of those supposedly 'liberated' but subjected to forced and unpaid labour that has been suppressed.[130]

In an article on the History Reclaimed group's website reproduced from the *Telegraph*, Nigel Biggar and Doug Stokes argue that 'woke' criticisms of the West's history undermine the liberalism upon which Westerners rely for their security and prosperity. Doug Stokes believes that drawing attention to the racism and violence of British colonialism, 'especially post George Floyd', 'has weakening effects for a very successful, multi-racial, liberal democracy. It's very divisive and it's playing people off against each other'.[131] Yet anti-'woke' rants like this are part of the backlash against precisely the most precious aspects of Western liberalism that have been won since 1945 — gains such as the civil rights of Black people.

History Reclaimed's current campaign (as of January 2022) is for censorship of the BBC. They have used the *Telegraph* and the *Spectator* to argue for a panel to police what the public broadcaster can say about the British Empire and its legacies, supposedly to prevent its being hijacked by 'woke' historians and commentators.[132] Again, such censorship strikes me as very far from defending the best traditions of Western liberalism.

In November 2021 I conducted what the historian of colonial violence Kim Wagner labelled a 'thought experiment' on Twitter. I was planning a new textbook on the British Empire for undergraduate students, based on the work of hundreds of colleagues who are also specialists, and on my own previous books. Since I did not want the book immediately to fall prey to the polarised responses

Academia

of a culture war, I asked some of the main protagonists of History Reclaimed if they might be willing to 'recognise some features of the British Empire that are incontrovertible: substantiated by a vast documentary record and agreed by the overwhelming majority of experts,' I asked, 'maybe we can find at least some common ground? Taking an overview of most of Britain's forty-odd crown and settler colonies as well as India, thinking of an extended ... period and being aware of exceptions', I proposed we might all agree that:

1. **British colonization involved great violence against people of colour.**
2. **Colonised people of colour were subordinated to White colonists — e.g. [they] had to show deference, [incurred] more severe judicial penalties, [experienced] restricted voting rights.**
3. **Most White Britons considered it common sense that they were superior to people of colour. Not necessarily biologically but culturally. An attitude that we call racism today.**
4. **As Empire retreated and Britons of colour came to [the] UK in greater numbers, they met a widespread view that Black citizens did not belong in Britain and faced racism, and**
5. **That right wing politicians have amplified and stoked this view of racially exclusive belonging beyond the end of Empire.**[133]

The polarisation that has already seeped into our view of the imperial past was evident in most of the responses from the History Reclaimed people that I had asked and their allies (mainly three anonymous accounts named after British East

India Company soldiers or authors). They sought to deflect the discussion into a cost-benefit argument about British rule in India specifically. There was particular insistence on the weight of evidence provided by the economic historian of India, Tirthankar Roy (cited above), who has analyzed data suggesting that Indian elites, and most notably merchants, benefited from the urbanisation, conflict-regulation and access to global markets secured by the East India Company. Despite Roy's recognition that data was lacking on how the mass of more ordinary Indians was affected by British rule, the inference drawn from his History Reclaimed readers was that the Empire as a whole must therefore have benefited the majority of people of colour in most other colonies.

Aside from this most substantive and persistent response, there was the rather rapid resort to personal insults that we have come to expect from social media. Once the attempts to deflect from the statements, rather than either challenge them with evidence or accept them had dried up, members of History Reclaimed and the anonymous accounts that amplified their voices resorted to comments about my arrogance in presuming to inform them about the empire and accused me of being racist for disagreeing with accounts set up by people of Asian descent.

Beyond the deficiencies of Twitter as a forum for serious debate, the exchange was enlightening about the methodology of denial that members of History Reclaimed and their politically-driven sympathisers tend to deploy when they present Britain's imperial history. In their determination to rebut evidence that racial distinction overwhelmingly structured the experience of colonialism, they follow the playbook of both Holocaust and climate change deniers. What Richard J Evans writes of David Irving, the holocaust denier, is just as true of those who evade the violence and racism of empire: 'The denial of history was the

Academia

product of political bias and political extremism, which had no place in the world of serious scholarship.'[134] Like Irving's account of the Second World War, as seen from Hitler and his associates' perspectives, the accounts of empire that have emanated from some of History Reclaimed's adherents have a 'curiously unreal quality: ... the atrocities, the sufferings of millions of people which were the result' of British colonialism, 'were not to be found.'[135]

Deniers attempt to cast doubt on the micro-data; on each individual piece of evidence in isolation, and stubbornly refuse to acknowledge what the aggregation of data tells us on a vast scale. They infer that because there's uncertainty over the precise construction of a gas chamber, or the rate of retreat of a particular glacier, the whole notion of the Holocaust or of climate change is debatable. For History Reclaimed members, because an official involved in a punitive expedition had an explanation for the killing of Africans (they were stamping out slavery, or they were preventing human sacrifice), or because certain classes of Indians did well out of Empire, the whole notion of colonial racial violence is deniable. Never mind the agglomerated data that one can access if one does collaborative research or reads the work of hundreds of colonial historians working in hundreds of archives with hundreds of thousands of sources over decades.

History Reclaimed's method reminds me of the defence barrister's arguments in a case on which I did jury service many years ago. The identification of an armed robber by multiple witnesses in an ID parade could have been mistaken; the number plate on the getaway car, taken down by a witness as it sped away, could have been bought randomly by someone else who affixed it to the same make, model and colour of car as the defendant's, and it could have been coincidental that the defendant had the same amount

Deny & Disavow

of money as that stolen, bundled in the same wrappers, under his bed. Clearly, the barrister argued, there was sufficient doubt to acquit! Fortunately, in that case the judge not only instructed the jury to ignore much of the defence case but also reprimanded the defence barrister for her more egregious flourishes such as the number plate 'coincidence'.

Patiently, a number of specialist historians have been trying to highlight History Reclaimed's more outrageous claims too. As with climate change, denial is becoming ever more difficult as the evidence mounts. Projects like the Legacies of British Slavery database and the East India Company at Home at UCL are the result of painstaking historical research over decades, inquiring into aspects of Britain's past that have been obscured or buried by previous generations of historians. The Legacies of British Slavery project, as we will see, has brought slavery home, using government registers to reveal how tens of thousands of ordinary Britons who had never seen an enslaved person in their lives nevertheless owned and profited from British subjects of colour at a distance. Each of us can find out who owned enslaved people in our own towns. They include, for instance, the vicar of my local church in East Sussex, and the man upon whose land my housing estate was built.[136]

The East India Company at Home project, meanwhile, has shown how Britons were rapacious in the eastern half of their empire too. Company shareholders based in villages, towns and cities across Britain, as we have seen, 'earned' dividends by charging Indians rent for the privilege of living on their own land. They also profited from illegal opium smuggling into China, using the proceeds to build some of our loveliest country estates, including those mentioned in the National Trust's report.[137]

Much of this historical work, revising what we thought

Academia

we knew of our imperial past, is now being popularised due to David Olusoga, British TV's first major Black historian, while *Empireland* author Sathnam Sanghera's mini-series *Empire State of Mind* has also threatened the monopoly that imperial nostalgia and self-congratulation once enjoyed on TV. Although both these presenters have met with torrents of racial abuse and threats, the members of History Reclaimed fear that they are swimming against a mounting current of publicly accessible historical research.

The recent research of two women in particular has incensed right wing culture warriors. The *Daily Mail* was obliged to pay £25,000 to the author Priyamvada Gopal, who has written about those who objected to imperialism at the time and entered the minefield of nativist emotions surrounding Winston Churchill. The newspaper had falsely accused her of inciting a race war in in article based on tweets that were actually mocked up by right wing trolls.[138] Corinne Fowler was the lead author of the National Trust report on slavery and colonialism. Her contribution has been referred to in the Common Sense group's manifesto as the epitome of hated historical revisionism. Nigel Biggar accessed the *Mail* to declare that 'The National Trust has shot itself in the foot … It has really got a lot of its members annoyed. I am one of them.'[139] He went on to ask, 'What motivates people like Professor Fowler to apparently see racism everywhere, even when it isn't there?' For someone who claims to know about history and feels entitled to use national media platforms to pronounce upon it, the denial that racism had anything to do with the proceeds from slave ownership is deeply concerning to colonial historians.

Academics and public commentators like Corinne Fowler, Priyamvada Gopal, Sathnam Sanghera and David Olusoga have been exposed to precisely what the Common

Deny & Disavow

Sense Group's Gareth Bacon alleges the 'woke' are doing: 'an explicit campaign of aggressive bullying, intimidation and censorship.' The Common Sense group approached the funders of Fowler's research project, announcing in the *Telegraph* that the project will receive no more public funding.[140] They then turned on a book that Fowler had published on colonial influences on the British countryside. One of the Common Sense Group authors, Lord Peter Lilley declared, 'If she cannot take criticism she should not be in the university, let alone lecturing the nation. Arguably, it is she who has insulted her country by her book whose very title — *Green Unpleasant Land* — tells us what she thinks of her fellow citizens.' And yet the Common Sense group, Restore Trust and History Reclaimed members complain that it is conservatives who are deprived of 'the right and the ability to challenge those on the left'; that 'any attempt to do so is viciously put down — disagreement is not now tolerated and any perceived deviation from the narrow 'true path' is ruthlessly crushed' through 'noplatforming' and the rise of the 'cancel culture'. Corrine Fowler herself notes, 'The heatedness of the recent media response ... shows just what is at stake: a selective vision of nation that underplays the impact of four colonial centuries, or a version that embraces a post-imperial ... "convivial culture".'[141]

Academic history, as History Reclaimed asserts, 'has become one of the major battlegrounds in the culture wars'. However, this is not because of specialist colonial historians' efforts to raise awareness of our past. It is because members of History Reclaimed along with allies in the Conservative Party, Restore Trust and the right wing press are determined to respond to Black Lives Matter protests by staking a defence of a racially unequal *status quo* on the ground of history. Perhaps the best critique of the History Reclaimed project

Academia

comes from the rhetoric of the group itself: 'Tendentious and even blatantly false readings of history are creating divisions, resentments, and even violence. This is damaging to democracy and to a free society.'

Part Three

Chapter Eight

Glaring Omissions

A Year in the Life of the British Empire

If the picture of the British Empire that populist culture warriors want to preserve in aspic is an unrealistic one, based on historic, self-congratulatory, White Britons' stories, how best might we understand it as a complex entity? Part of the problem — the reason that populist culture warriors can make so much headway among contributors to the *MailOnline* comments section, for example — is profound ignorance among Britons about the realities of the British Empire.

The Tudors, who ruled England for around a century four hundred years ago, bizarrely, get more attention in our National Curriculum than the British Empire, which ruled a significant portion of the world for around three hundred years, came to an end only in my parents' generation, and shaped modern Britain fundamentally. So what should British children be taught about the Empire?

The problem with any glib characterisation of the relationship between Empire and race is that the Empire was not only vast and diverse, but constantly changing. It consisted of several projects pursued by Britons and others simultaneously across the world. Some of these projects were mutually reinforcing, such as when Manchester's textile manufacturers aligned with Palmerston's government in pursuing the populist Second Opium War. Some of them were contradictory, such as when missionaries sought to halt the advance of British colonisation in New Zealand on the grounds that settlers would corrupt the pure civilising and Christianising influence of the missionaries among the Māori.

We have to start somewhere, though, so I'll start with a snapshot of the Empire in 1838, a year that apologists for the Empire might set as its moral reset button — when the unpaid apprenticeships succeeding slavery finally ended, and when Queen Victoria's coronation took place. In the culture warriors' narrative, this is the point at which the British Empire started to do better, having acknowledged and atoned for its guilt when it came to slavery to the West and the plunder of India to the East.

A snapshot of the British Empire in all its range and diversity in 1838 gives some indication of the aspects of Britain's past, at home and overseas, that we need to start teaching if we're to move beyond the complacent narratives of the last 100 years, and beyond slavery as the main signifier of colonialism as a whole.

1838: A Year in the Empire [142]

When James Stephen, permanent under-secretary at the Colonial Office, arrived at his desk on 1 January 1838, he was confronted by piles of despatches from across the world. Stephen spent every day 'diligently … keeping back the flood of papers from deluging us,' warning his sister that 'I shall soon become a mere bit of blotting paper myself!' Amidst letters from imperial governors in Australia, southern Africa, Sierra

Glaring Omissions

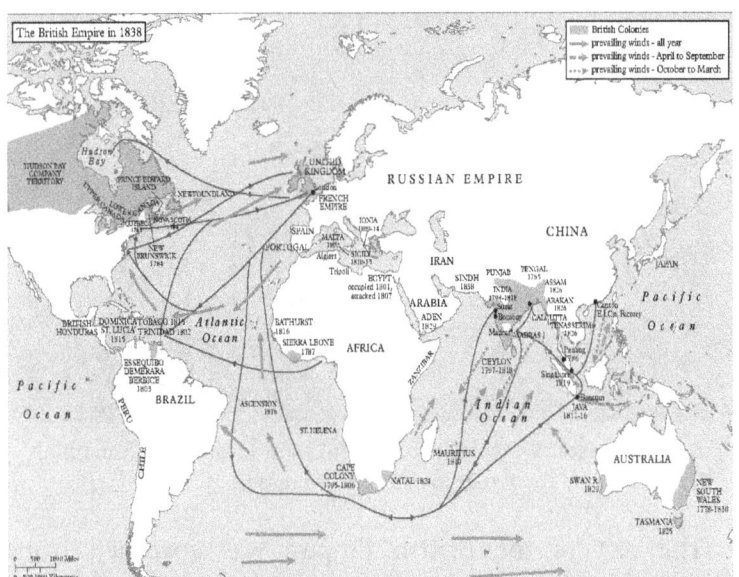

Map of the British Empire in 1838. Alan Lester, Kate Boehme and Peter Mitchell, *Ruling the World: Freedom, Civilisation and Liberalism in the Nineteenth Century British Empire* (Cambridge University Press, 2021).

Leone, Malta and Heligoland (in the North Sea) was a particularly worrying one about a colonists' rebellion in Upper Canada.

Stephen was the personification of the Colonial Office, working eighteen-hour days, six days a week to interpret every dispatch and draft most of the responses on behalf of the British government. He and his twenty-five staff worked from a dilapidated townhouse in Downing Street, its floors creaking under the weight of filing cabinets. The journalist and MP Charles Buller wrote of its 'sighing rooms', where supplicants waited endlessly for appointments in dark, dingy annexes, providing Charles Dickens with a model for Little Dorrit's 'circumlocution office'. From this building, thirty-two Crown colonies were administered.

Deny & Disavow

East India House (demolished in 1861) was located in Leadenhall Street in the City of London.

The rest of the British Empire was governed from East India House, a much grander neo-classical palace in the heart of the financial district. Here the East India Company's directors oversaw the governance of India and associated territories with a staff three times as large as Stephen's. In 1838 the government's Board of Control, which had supervised the Company since the days of scandal associated with Clive and the nabobs, was housed in a nondescript townhouse in Westminster. It was headed by John Cam Hobhouse, a friend of Lord Byron who had spent time in jail for radical pamphleteering in his youth but was now a considerably mellowed Whig MP.

Stephen's worrying despatch from Canada had been written in November 1837 and taken over a month to reach London. Steamships were in their infancy and the vagaries of ocean current, and wind determined sailing times. When William Nicolay, governor of Mauritius, complained that he had still not been notified officially of Queen Victoria's accession back in June 1837, although the news had already

Glaring Omissions

arrived with the London newspapers, Stephen explained tersely that 'Merchant Vessels are simultaneously advertised as about to sail from London, Liverpool, Bristol, Glasgow ... and ... the actual time of their departure cannot be stated with any degree of certainty, until immediately before they sail ... Moreover ... vessels do not arrive at their destination in the order ... in which they may have... left England.'

Hobhouse's communications were no more reliable. The quickest route for despatches from India was from Bombay (Mumbai) or Karachi via the Red Sea, across the Isthmus of Suez by land and on by sea from Alexandria. With sailing ships frequently becalmed in the Red Sea, the Company was a pioneer investor in steamships. In January its agent in Alexandria negotiated access to coal depots at Ottoman ports en route. Despatches sent from East India House in March 1838 would reach Bombay in a record forty-one days.

Given its dispersed nature, its fragmented administration and the difficulties of communication, how was the largest empire that the world had ever seen governed, everywhere and all at once? I'll proceed month by month to give an idea of the scope and diversity of this Empire, but also of its persistently racialised nature.

January-April

On 1 January, Lord Auckland, the East India Company's governor general, and his sister Emily were diverted from touring northern India by reports of an unusually severe famine in the Agra region. The economic volatility brought by the end of the Company's monopoly on trade in 1833 had contributed to extreme poverty. Indian producers reliant on cotton production and export had been undercut by British imports. In return for abolishing their monopoly, as we have seen, parliament had guaranteed the Company's shareholders annual dividends of 10.5 per cent, derived wholly from the rent charged to Indians. This was not helping impoverished peasants to buy food. El Niño weather events had then caused harvest failure, further raising prices.

Hobhouse received Auckland's 'harrowing accounts of famine and distress' in February. He and the Company directors agreed a sum of Rs 2 million for the able-bodied who could work for it but prohibited handouts to the incapacitated to afford 'the greatest possible facilities for free and unrestricted commerce'. In all, some 800,000 Indians would starve to death by the end of the summer. The Company's investments in steam, meanwhile, were laying the foundations for steamship navigation of the major rivers and railway development on behalf of British investors, underwritten by Indian taxpayers.

Meanwhile, Stephen was dealing with the aftermath of abolishing slavery. The Antislavery Act of 1833, which he had drafted, had not actually freed enslaved people from their owners' control. Instead, 800,000 enslaved people had become unpaid 'apprentices', obliged to continue working for their former owners, and subject to corporal punishment if they disobeyed. This period of 'apprenticeship', along with the payment of £20 million compensation to the slave owners (not the enslaved), had been necessary to secure parliament's approval for abolition. Apprentices were due to be freed to find their own employers from 1 August this year.

One unanticipated effect of emancipation was in the Cape Colony at the southern tip of Africa. There, more Afrikaner (Boer) colonists were prompted to move across the northern frontier on what later historians called the Great Trek, preferring continued expansion and self-rule to a new form of British governance that threatened their ownership of enslaved people. On the colony's eastern

Glaring Omissions

frontier, Governor Benjamin D'Urban's recent annexation of further Xhosa land for British settlers had been disallowed and the Lieutenant governor, Andries Stockenström, was maintaining peace through treaties with the amaXhosa. However, he would be sacked within a year as a result of British settlers' lobbying in favour of continued expansion and Xhosa dispossession.

Meanwhile the British colony of Sierra Leone was still the main dropping off point for Africans rescued by the Royal Navy from other nations' slave ships. The West Africa squadron, as we have seen, had been set up to suppress other countries' slave trading once Britain had abolished its own in 1807. More than 1,500 British sailors would die as they captured 1,600 slave ships and freed 150,000 Africans from enslavement between 1808 and 1860.

Traditionally referred to as 'Liberated Africans', the Africans freed from captured ships are now generally referred to as 'Recaptives'. Even those taken back to Africa by the Royal Navy, rather than left in the Caribbean or St Helena, were generally unable to return home. Some were assigned as free labour to colonists in the Cape Colony, but most taken to Freetown in Sierra Leone. From there it was all but impossible to return home across hundreds of miles of unknown territory infested with slave raiders. Most were assigned to free settlers in the colony, both Black and White, for 10–15 years, as unpaid 'apprentices'.

Critics of the assignment system for 'liberated Africans' alleged that they were simply transferred from one form of slavery to another. 'Runaway' apprentices were sought in Sierra Leone's newspapers in the same way as enslaved escapees were in the colonies they were being taken to as slaves until the Royal Navy rescued them. Among them, however, were also others who found benefactors willing

Glaring Omissions

to help them integrate as free settlers themselves. One such was Ajayi, whose patron educated him in England. He became Samuel Crowther, the first African Bishop in West Africa.

The emancipation of those formerly held in slavery in 1838 would bring a significant increase in the free Black population of Jamaica, potentially eligible to vote for its Assembly. Governor Lionel Smith had a suggestion — that the property qualification be raised in anticipation, to maintain White planter domination. From Mauritius, Governor Nicolay agreed: 'The period is far — very far — distant', when a 'representative legislature could be safely introduced, founded on ... the equality of legal rights' for the colony's people of colour.

Stephen affirmed that any explicit racial discrimination could not be allowed. Setting a precedent for other colonies where property-less, formerly enslaved people of colour were about to join the predominantly White free population, the Jamaican Assembly would raise the property franchise without specifying any form of racial exclusion. After the Morant Bay former-slave rebellion in 1865 this oldest colonial assembly would vote to dissolve itself and be ruled direct from London again rather than face the prospect of further Black encroachment on government.

Stephen's overriding concern, however, was not the rights of the newly freed Black population of the Caribbean, but the rebellion of White settlers in Canada. British settlers in Upper Canada were joining with French-speaking colonists in Lower Canada to force the governors' cliques in each of the separate colonies to share power. Armed US citizens were raiding across the border in support of the rebels and Stephen feared an American Revolution II. 'Oh Canada' he lamented, 'what wrongs have I done thee that thou ... pursuest me in my house & my office, my walks & my dreams?' The rebellion was a by-product of decades encouraging Britons to emigrate to the colonies of North America, Australia and southern Africa as a cure for supposed overpopulation at home. Turbo-charged 'systematic colonization', as advocated by the serial heiress abductee Edward Gibbon Wakefield, was now government policy.

The accelerated British diaspora, which would amount to twenty million over the course of the century, was causing Stephen two major headaches. The first, manifested in Canada, was how to respond when British settlers overseas demanded the right to govern themselves. The other was how these settlers should engage with the indigenous peoples whose lands they were taking. Stephen was simultaneously digesting the recommendations of a select committee, comprised largely of those who had campaigned against slavery, which condemned emigrants for the brutality of their invasion. He agreed that the Christianity and 'civilization' of indigenous peoples should be the objects of British colonization, not their destruction. Yet he still had to encourage further emigration.

As indigenous Haudenosaunee were helping the loyalist militia round up the cross-border raiders in Canada, Aboriginal dispossession was proceeding at an alarming rate in Australia. From Sydney, New South Wales' Governor Richard Bourke notified Stephen that he had sent a magistrate after Britons who had taken it upon themselves to settle around Geelong. He placed 'the greatest reliance on [the] ... humanity, good temper, and considerate disposition' of Foster Fyans. In reality 'Flogger Fyans' systematically acquitted settlers accused of killing Aboriginal people, declaring that 'the only plan ... is to ... deal with such useless savages on the spot.' The rapid colonisation of the Port Phillip District (now Victoria), including by Britons who had recently been awarded compensation for the loss

Glaring Omissions

of enslaved people in the Caribbean, continued as Kulin peoples' lands were filled with pastoralists. Despite the arrival of a handful of Protectors of Aborigines, appointed to safeguard the interests of Aboriginal people, the Aboriginal population is estimated to have declined by 90 per cent over the ensuing decade.

In March, George Gipps replaced Bourke. The agenda for Gipps' first advisory council meeting included Stephen's instructions for 'the just and humane treatment of the aborigines' alongside a report from Major Nunn who, in January, had led a military force killing over forty Kaamilaraay men, women and children accused of spearing settlers' invasive sheep. Stephen was at a loss to advise the new governor exactly how he should show 'humanity' to Aboriginal people while encouraging British settlement on their land.

May–August

The British Empire's character was determined not just by Britons' relations with those they colonised, but also by the grand geopolitics of the age. Rivalry with Russia was often a key determinant of imperial policy since Russian imperial expansion in Central Asia was seen as threatening British control of India. Here the Foreign Office proved as influential in imperial policymaking as either the Colonial Office or East India Company. In May, at the Board of Control, Hobhouse panicked upon hearing that a Russian envoy had entered Kabul to attempt an alliance with the Afghan Amir, Dost Mohammad. The Foreign Office dictated that the Company participate in the 'Great Game' contesting any Russian encroachment on the borders of India.

The Company's agent in Kabul believed that the

independent-minded Amir had no intention of indulging the Russians, but the Company's Governor General Lord Auckland, and Hobhouse, were falling under the spell of a rival advisor, William Hay Macnaghten. His suggestion was to use Company forces to overthrow Dost Mohammad and reinstate a compliant former Amir, Shah Shuja. This would be regime change in the interests of British strategy.

As Hobhouse and the Company Directors schemed to secure a puppet regime in Afghanistan, over at the Colonial Office Stephen remained preoccupied with Canada. Against his wishes, the government had decided to send out Lord Durham as an appeaser to the rebels. He arrived in May and proposed later that year that the Canadian settlers be granted representative government, based on a low property franchise. It would mean that most White men would be able to elect their own government, with only external relations reserved for Colonial Office control. Devised while franchise qualifications were being raised to exclude free people of colour elsewhere, this solution would maintain British emigrants' sense of belonging to the empire. It would be emulated in due course in the Australian colonies, New Zealand, the Cape Colony and Natal.

In June, Gipps reported that another massacre of Australian Aboriginal people had been committed at Myall Creek. For the first time, White witnesses were willing to testify to seeing the partially burnt corpses of twenty-eight Wirrayaraay women, children and elderly men. Governor Gipps saw an opportunity to demonstrate humanitarian resolve, ensuring a retrial after a settler jury's initial acquittal of the culprits. However, once seven of the murderers were hanged, previously divided former convict and free settlers united to press for Canadian-style self-governance, not least so that Australia could be 'cleared' for settlement without further philanthropic interference from London. Despite

Glaring Omissions

mounting evidence of the regularity and toll on Aboriginal society of massacres like that at Myall Creek, disputing their existence has been one of the main activities of Australia's own culture warriors since the late 1980s.[143]

Meanwhile the philanthropic impulse that had driven the anti-slavery campaign found its fulfilment as formerly enslaved 'apprentices' around the empire were at last able to seek paid employment from 1st August. Many were able to find employment but were expected to pay for the first time for plantation accommodation with minimal wages and no capital of their own. The first impulse for many others was to reunite with family members dispersed among different 'owners' and find land upon which they could derive a subsistence together, depriving their former owners of labour. This happened both in some of the Caribbean colonies and the Cape Colony. Former apprentices found it more difficult to either acquire land or compete with cheaper Indian workers brought into Mauritius.

At the same time, the former owners of enslaved people were investing the compensation money that they had received from the British government for the loss of their 'property'. Some put it into railways, banks and insurance companies in Britain, helping to fuel the industrial revolution. Others looked across the Empire for opportunities. Some former slave owners stayed in the Caribbean and Central America, bringing indentured workers from India to replace lost slave labour, while others re-invested in new zones of imperial expansion, especially in the burgeoning Australian, southern African and North American colonies, and New Zealand. The new colony of South Australia was funded in part from compensation pay-outs to the slave owners of the Caribbean, while the colonisation of Western Australia and Victoria was also propelled by former slave-owners.[144] In South Africa, much of the compensation

Deny & Disavow

money found its way into banks supporting former slave owners' agriculture and the expansion of White colonisation in the eastern Cape. 'This enabled planters and farmers to ride out emancipation with far fewer changes to the wider societies and economies of the former slave colonies than humanitarians and abolitionists had hoped'. The Bank of South Africa, founded in 1838, had 2,050 shareholders of whom at least 951 were slave-owners, investing some of the £2.6 million in compensation for the 11,896 slaves they had owned.[145] Many of those Britons formerly invested in slavery simply adapted to new forms of conquest and exploitation after abolition in other parts of the Empire, aided by the compensation that the British government awarded them.

September–December

During September the Foreign Office persuaded Russia to back away from potential conflict in Afghanistan. However, the Governor General in Calcutta, Lord Auckland, was committed to conflict before he could be called off. On 1st October, he issued the Simla Declaration, pledging to restore Shah Shuja to the throne in Afghanistan with help from Ranjit Singh's Sikh kingdom. Hobson doctored the Kabul agent's despatches to back the governor general in London. Auckland's sister Emily sighed, 'poor, dear peaceful George had gone to war. Rather an inconsistency in his character'.

No sooner had Hobhouse committed the government to an unnecessary and ultimately disastrous invasion of Afghanistan than he was confronted by the next crisis. This was the First Opium War, fought as we have seen, to impose British opium smuggling from India to China. As we saw from Wolseley's career, it would not be the last.

Each of the events in this Empire of 1838 had a

Glaring Omissions

background in previous developments and repercussions in the years following. Regime change was soon accomplished in Afghanistan, with the first of what would turn out to be three British occupations in 1839, but the 'stupidity' of Macnaghten's plan (the description was the Duke of Wellington's) was revealed thereafter. Shah Shuja, a puppet whose strings were pulled by infidel foreigners, was never going to become acceptable to Afghanistan's tribal leaders. Fighters lining the Hindu Kush's narrow passes cut off supplies and reinforcements to the army supporting Britain's favoured ruler. In 1842 the beleaguered and starving Anglo-Indian garrison accepted an offer of safe passage out, but nearly all were killed as they retreated, Hobhouse's nephew among them.

In China, in the meantime, the defeat of the Qing Empire launched China's 'century of humiliation', for which it is now making amends. For successive Chinese Communist Party leaders, the lessons from the period of unequal treaties imposed by European colonial powers, and then Japan since the Opium Wars, have included the need to industrialise independently, to support anti-colonial movements and post-colonial governments in Africa and Asia (and encourage dependency on China instead), and to resist unequal trade deals with the West.[146]

In drafting the act ending slavery back in 1833, Stephen had helped bring one kind of British Empire to an end, but he admitted that in the post-emancipation empire of 1838, the devastating impact of colonization on indigenous societies was 'clear and irremediable; nor do I suppose it is possible to discover any method by which the impending Catastrophe, namely the extermination of the Black Race can long be avoided'. Assertions from its contemporary defenders that the end of slavery saw the Empire's moral rejuvenation were thus disputed at the time, by the man responsible for administering most of it.

At the same time, Stephen was helping devise the means for replacing enslaved peoples' labour. The scene of greatest planter anxiety about the emancipation of formerly enslaved 'apprentices' was the Caribbean. Jamaican planters were proposing schemes to secure replacement cheap labour from other colonies including Malta, before William Ewart Gladstone's father set a precedent in Guyana: importing indentured labourers from British India.

In Mauritius, impoverished peasants brought by the new steamships from India, were already providing planters with cheaper labour than formerly enslaved apprentices. Many of these were being thrown off estates even while their owners were receiving compensation for their emancipation. From the 1840s onwards, the Colonial Office would liaise with the East India Company (the India Office after the 1857 Uprising) to build an indentured labour system which yielded a diaspora of over half a million Indians, or 'coolies' as the British called them, for Britons' plantations in Central America, the Caribbean, southern Africa and the Pacific.

The new British Empire of 1838 developed a template through which people of colour with lesser civil rights, would continue to supply cheap labour to White Britons, prompting demographic shifts around the world. One consequence of this new global labour redistribution regime was greater integration of the British Empire's administrative offices. With the India Office now playing a role in the allocation of cheap labour to Britons in the Crown and settler colonies, from the late 1860s, it was placed in a wing adjoining the Colonial Office in a new, purposely designed government building in King Charles Street, Westminster, now the Foreign, Commonwealth and Development Office.

Chapter Nine

India and the Settler Colonies

The Raj

There has long been a debate about whether British rule was good for India and Indians as well as for Britons. Claiming that it was generally of benefit to Indians is one of the strongest cards played by those who strive to deny the racism of Empire as a whole. We have seen that, in the late eighteenth century, even the majority of informed Britons themselves believed that a relatively wealthy subcontinent was being plundered for Britons' benefit, but what about during the nineteenth century, by which time a Board of Control had parliamentary oversight of the Company's activities and the Company and later Raj (British government structure succeeding the Company) was investing in irrigation, railways, steam navigation, schools, colleges and new legal structures? Surely these must have benefitted Indians too?

Some Indians did indeed benefit. Wealthier Indians themselves invested in these activities and some, such as the rulers of Awadh, displaced by the British in the run up to the 1857 Uprising, were even Company shareholders. As we have seen, the Uprising was prompted in part by the new alliance forming between Indian merchants and British rulers, which excluded the established aristocracy. In the wake of the Uprising Indian elites took advantage of the new trade networks, urban growth and relative security afforded by British control. One lesson learned by the Governor General, Charles Canning (derided by some as 'clemency Canning') was the need to resume alliances with the rulers of the princely states — those internally self-governing territories that Dalhousie had not already absorbed — too.

Displays of the Indian aristocracy's wealth and grandeur, underpinned by ultimate British authority, became a key motif of the Raj from 1857 until independence. However, the lavishly catered Durbar in Delhi to cement the Raj's alliance with princely rulers in celebration of Queen Victoria's new title Empress of India in 1877 took place, obscenely as far as many British observers were concerned, while millions of her subjects were starving in another famine which the British government felt no responsibility to alleviate beyond relief work for the able bodied.

As the British government in India adapted to survive after the Uprising, the educated Indian middle classes also seized new opportunities to join the lower tiers of the governmental apparatus. As elsewhere in the Empire, some indigenous groups benefited from alliances with their alien rulers, or from opportunities to enhance their standing relative to others, including traditional enemies. Answering the question as to whether, overall, British rule was good or bad for India, however, is a much trickier matter, for two main reasons. First, there is a lack of data on most of the Indian population, who were not of the middle class or elite. Secondly, isolating and assessing the impact of British rule involves a counterfactual. We would need to know how Indian society would have developed in the absence of the British, and that, of course, is impossible to ascertain. Would the various governmental entities in India at the time of Clive's victory at Plassey have agglomerated to form

India and the Settler Colonies

an updated version of the Mughal Empire, perhaps led by the Marathas, for instance, or would the disintegration of a centralised authority over much of the subcontinent have continued for many decades? Would an emerging alternative authority have embarked on a programme equivalent to that of the Meiji restoration from 1868 in Japan, cherry picking the best aspects of European and American economic and social developments without surrendering sovereignty, and investing for domestic rather than British purposes? As Amartya Sen puts it, 'Japan did not stand still' in the absence of colonial rule; 'nor would India have done so'. Sen continues, 'the Japanese went straight to learning from the west without being subjected to imperialism. They sent people for training in the US and Europe and made institutional changes that were clearly inspired by western experience. They did not wait to be coercively globalised via imperialism.'[147]

We simply have no way of knowing what would have happened in India without Britain's self-interested rule. What we do know is that, by the mid-nineteenth century, a group of British-educated Indians appreciated the potential freedoms articulated by British liberal writers and espoused by their rulers. At the same time though, they deeply resented their exclusion from the opportunity to shape the governance of their own country alongside the British and following the precepts of non-racial liberalism articulated by them. The Indian nationalist movement of the late nineteenth century was driven above all by the hypocrisy of a supposedly universal liberalism that in fact excluded people of colour.[148] As Secretary of State for India Lord Salisbury commented, 'If England was to remain supreme ... she must tolerate the political role of Indian princes and of participation by Indians in the administration, but ... if the number of well-educated Indians ... should increase, the government would face the indecent and embarrassing necessity of closing that avenue to them'.[149]

It was not until 1892 that 39 Indians could be elected to the imperial and provincial legislative councils, rising to 139 in 1909. These were chosen by a few Indian electors as representatives of specific religious and social groups and remained purely advisory. This was the extent of the democracy that British rule brought to India before the First World War, and even this concession was in response to mounting nationalist anger.[150] The principle articulated by Macaulay in 1833 held firm: Indians were racially unsuited to govern themselves or to play anything more than a minor role in assisting the British to rule over their compatriots.

Britain, however, was able to continue benefiting not only from rent extraction from its Indian subjects and commercial opportunities in India, but also from its vast armies. Indian troops were deployed on behalf of Britain and its empire throughout the later nineteenth century and on into the First and Second World Wars. As the recent scandal over the lack of commemoration of Black and Indian soldiers reveals, their lives were seen to matter somewhat less than those of the White troops killed in these campaigns.[151] The same can be said of the famine victims of 1876–9 and 1943. It is simply inconceivable that the British government would have tolerated the death of around 3 million White British subjects, wherever they lived, even during World War II. There have been no Indian famines on the scale of those under British rule since the British left in 1947.

As I will argue below, any overall balance sheet approach to the costs and benefits of empire is meaningless when

India and the Settler Colonies

those costs and benefits were felt so unevenly by different kinds of imperial subject, but it is worth noting the point made by William Dalrymple that in '1600, when the East India Company was founded, Britain was generating 1.8% of the world's GDP, while India was producing 22.5%. By the peak of the Raj, those figures had more or less been reversed: India was reduced from the world's leading manufacturing nation to a symbol of famine and deprivation'.[152] The relative changes in GDP share were not all due to British rule. The USA, other European countries and other empires were industrialising and gaining a greater share of global GDP during this period. But what seems clear is that the British rule of India benefited many Britons more than it did the mass of Indians.

While princely and merchant allies of the Raj could be further enriched and celebrated by the British, and the well-educated elite could be absorbed into its bureaucracy and judiciary up to a certain point, life expectancy at birth in India as the Raj ended was around 32 years and adult literacy was barely 15 per cent. As Tirthankar Roy puts it, 'British rule's effect upon strengthening markets ... was far greater than its impact on public welfare. Markets favour the capitalist and those with goods and services to sell; markets can be inequalizing. The Company's legacy was greater inequality between capitalists and skilled workers on the one side and unskilled or manual workers on the other. Merchants ... gained; the south Indian farm servant did not gain much ... The colonial state had neither the will nor the money to make a significant difference to peasants and labourers'.[153]

The British government of India lacked the money to improve conditions of the masses in part because the British

Treasury itself was still subsidized by the rent extracted from India. In 1884 Richard Temple presented the 'General Statistics of the British Empire' to the Royal Statistical Society, noting that of the £203 million at the disposal of the British state for general government within the United Kingdom, £89 million came from the UK itself (including Ireland), £74 million from India, and £40 million from territories and colonies in the rest of empire.[154]

Perhaps the most beneficial legacy of British rule in India is a multiparty democracy and a free press, but these were denied to Indians rather than offered them by the British. Post-independence governments made them available to the masses only when the British left. As Sen notes, 'they were the fruits of learning from Britain's own experience, which India could use freely only after the period of empire had ended. Imperial rule tends to require some degree of tyranny ... to keep colonial subjects in check ... These freedom-oriented institutions were for the rulers but not for the imperial subjects.'[155]

The Settler and Crown Colonies

As we have seen from our 1838 snapshot, during the nineteenth and early twentieth centuries some twenty million Britons assumed the right to settle on indigenous peoples' land in North America, southern Africa and Australasia, coming massively to outnumber the surviving indigenous peoples in all but southern Africa. They came from the full spectrum of British classes. Some were aristocrats and members of the gentry trying to enlarge or protect their wealth. Others were members of the middle classes doing well enough to fund their own emigration in the expectation of becoming landowners, farmers, or more prosperous members of the burgeoning colonial middle

India and the Settler Colonies

classes. Many were pauper emigrants, able to emigrate only with the assistance of local and central governments seeking to relieve British taxpayers of the burden of looking after them. The largest share went to the now independent USA, but most of those who emigrated to the British colonies continued to consider themselves Britons until the twentieth century.

Inevitably these Britons encountered indigenous peoples seeking to defend their land from invasion, as we have already seen in the case of Australia in 1838. Yet, settlers saw self-defence as a sign of savagery — an inability to accept the inevitability of a superior race spreading itself across the world. There were moments, especially in the 1830s, where assumptions that 'natives' or 'aboriginals' could legitimately be swept aside were challenged vocally by philanthropists. But the terms in which they objected are telling of the way that most Britons thought about race right up until the aftermath of World War II.

Anyone who has immersed themselves in the letters, diaries, memoirs and despatches of British colonists knows that they shared a 'common sense' understanding of racial difference with most Britons who stayed at home. White British people were superior to people of colour. Britons' sense of entitlement to colonise and govern others — even their obligation to intervene against slavery and barbarism on behalf of 'weaker' people — was based upon this superiority. Those who deny this unshakeable conviction of racial superiority can only have read the archival record of Empire, if they have read it at all, wearing ideological blinkers.

The more philanthropic among Victorian Britons, including James Stephen at the Colonial Office, believed that White superiority was not inherent but acquired. Black people's inferiority was due to nurture rather than nature.

Deny & Disavow

These more progressive Britons were mainly evangelical Christians. They wanted to act as benevolent instructors, enabling people of colour to bridge the gap and become 'more like us', in religion and in culture. British rule was required to create the right environment for that transformation.

This more philanthropic view of race was articulated most influentially by a Parliamentary Committee on empire, set up in 1835 and chaired by the man who had taken the antislavery campaign over from William Wilberforce, Thomas Fowell Buxton (whose memorial fountain we saw earlier). Buxton's committee provided a scathing commentary on the abuses of indigenous peoples and was deeply resented by settlers overseas. It reported in 1837 that 'The British Empire has been signally blessed by Providence'. God had granted Britain 'her wealth her prosperity, her intellectual, her moral and her religious advantages' in order to 'carry civilization and humanity, peace and good government, and, above all, the knowledge of the true God, to the uttermost ends of the earth'.[156]

Indigenous Black and brown people, these 'progressives' of their day insisted, were not biologically deficient; rather they lagged behind White Europeans for want of tutelage. The former Attorney General of New South Wales, Henry Saxe Bannister, explained why this rendered Empire an obligation, or what Kipling would later call 'The white man's burden': 'If we, the civilised, could not, physically, exist in the same land with the barbarian and the savage without destroying them, it would be a paramount duty to discourage the extension of colonies', he admitted. However British colonisation was justified, because 'we must not despair of raising the most simple to the true point of political well-being.'[157]

The more reactionary among our nineteenth century forebears disagreed that people of colour would ever be

India and the Settler Colonies

capable of attaining that point. Abolitionists had campaigned for the emancipation of enslaved people on the grounds that only when freed could they become civilised, under British tutelage. Slave owners and their allies countered with the assertion that racial characteristics not only determined intelligence, imagination, the ability to work for future gain and all sorts of other attributes, but that these characteristics were fixed, immutable. Racial differences were a matter of nature, not nurture.

Emancipation would be a failure in this view because Africans were congenitally incapable of European achievements — something which later racial scientists colluded in 'verifying'. Once freed, these racial pessimists believed, enslaved Black people would simply revert to savagery. The only thing to do was to keep them in their place, controlling them for the greater good, using overwhelming violence whenever necessary. With the expansion of colonisation this applied to indigenous people too.

At the extreme, some Britons believed that acts of extermination, or genocide of 'savage' peoples, were perfectly reasonable, if not unavoidable. The letters of a British settler in South Africa, John Mitford Bowker, published in 1864, are revealing. He lamented that 'The day was when our plains were covered with tens of thousands of springboks; they are gone now'. Despite the fact that the species' disappearance was entirely due to Bowker and other British emigrants' over-hunting and displacement with sheep, he continued, 'my heart yearns towards them, and I regret that so much innocent beauty, elegance and agility must needs be swept from the Earth'. However, Bowker continued, 'My feelings towards the Kafir (derogatory term for the Xhosa people) are not of that stamp. I know that he has disregarded the zealous missionary for years … I know him to be the great bar to all improvement amongst us. I know that rapine and murder are in all his thoughts, and I see them in his looks, and I hate him accordingly ... and I begin to think that he too, as well as the springbok, must give place ... Is it just that a few thousand worthless savages are to sit like a nightmare upon a land that would support millions of civilised men happily? Nay, heaven forbids it.'[158]

Well-meant Genocide

There was never an official policy of genocide, as in the mass eradication by killing, in Britain's settler colonies. A more accurate description is cultural genocide — the attempt to eradicate a people's way of life. Emulating the British, it was a policy adopted by the US Army General Richard Henry Pratt against Native Americans. He described the intent: to 'kill the Indian and save the man'. It was an approach which provided something of a middle ground between Saxe Bannister's humanitarian approach to empire and Bowker's exterminatory one.

Indigenous societies would cease to exist, but patiently, over the course of a generation or two. The means would be the forcible fostering and adoption of indigenous families' children and their removal from the supposed pernicious influence of their own culture. Brought up in White-run residential schools and fostered to White families far from the indigenous reserves, they would go on to 'assimilate' or 'amalgamate', marrying White partners and producing Whiter children with each subsequent generation. Their parents' 'full blooded' aboriginal generation would be left to wither away out of sight in the reserves. After a few decades, administrators hoped, no one who was distinctively indigenous, either in appearance or in culture, would remain.

India and the Settler Colonies

Such civilising experiments or cultural genocidal policies, depending on how you look at it, were first ventured with the enthusiastic participation of settler missionaries and churches in Australia and Canada. Indigenous children were routinely taken away from their families simply for being indigenous and subjected to boarding schools and foster families where many were neglected and abused. In Canada, British colonial policies sent 150,000 children to 139 residential schools, where more than 4,000 died of disease and neglect.[159] In July 2021, some of the legacies came home to roost when over 1,000 unmarked First Nations children's graves were found and protestors defaced or toppled statues of Queens Victoria and Elizabeth II in anger.

I viscerally recall my first experience of working on the newly digitised archive of one of these institutions — the Anglican-run Sarcee Indian School.[160] Canada's Department of Indian Affairs had instructed the school 'to provide … religious instruction at proper times; to instruct the male pupils … in gardening, farming, and care of stock … to instruct the female pupils in cooking, laundry work, needlework, general housewifery and dairy work … to teach all pupils … English … calisthenics, physical drill and fire drill; to teach the effects of alcoholic drinks and narcotics on the human system … to instruct the older … pupils in the duties and privileges of British citizenship … training them in such knowledge and appreciation of Canada as will inspire them with respect and affection for the country and its laws'. The school's 'civilizing' mission did not end with the discharge of its pupils once they became teenagers, however. In 1914 it was instructed by the Department of Indian Affairs that 'Indian agents should carefully select the most favourable location for ex-pupils … removed to some extent from the older Indians' with 'most careful thought

Deny & Disavow

... given to the future of female pupils ... protected as far as possible from temptations to which they are often exposed. They will be assisted in any effort to become self-supporting, or helpful to their parents, or at the time of their marriage'.

The often-appalling conditions and fates of children subjected to these institutions are detailed in the medical reports from the Sarcee school, whose pupils suffered from regular outbreaks of tuberculosis between 1914 and the early 1920s. On 28th April 1917, the principal reported to the Department of Indian Affairs in Ottawa that the 'death of another pupil, #48 ... has caused a great deal of dissatisfaction among the Indians that this boy was not allowed to go home and it is going to make it more difficult for us to obtain fresh pupils'. On Feb. 17th, the Department wrote back that, despite the fact that Sarcee mothers were clamouring at the school gates and writing letters pleading for their children's return home to escape the epidemic, the school was correct not to oblige because it was more hygienic than their 'Indian' homes and had a nurse on site to offer better care.

With tuberculosis passed from one infected pupil to another through droplets from coughs and sneezes, this confinement was actually a death sentence for many pupils. Contradicting the rather sanguine reports of the resident nurse, Dr Corbett's inspection report of Nov. 1920 noted that of seventeen pupils remaining, all but four had tuberculosis. 'The condition of one little girl found in the infirmary', he wrote, 'is pitiable indeed. She lies curled up in a bed that is filthy, in a room that is untidy, dirty and dilapidated, in a northwest corner of the building with no provision of a balcony, sunshine or fresh air. Both sides of her neck and chest are swollen and five foul ulcers are discovered when we lift the bandages. This gives her pain and her tears from

India and the Settler Colonies

her fear of being touched intensifies the picture of her misery ... the general condition of nearly all the pupils is much below even a passable standard of health'. At least three pupils died at the school during that year alone, due to the settler authorities' sense of medical and civilizational superiority, and their obligation to abide by British colonial policies of forced assimilation.

In Australia, the British colonial policies of taking Aboriginal children from their families continued into the 1970s. Those affected are known as the Stolen Generation and they continue to experience the effects. 'Removal from their families affected all aspects of their lives. Some are still searching for their parents, others never succeeded as parents themselves and turned to substance abuse. Many feel that they are living a life surrounded by ghosts — people they don't know, but should'.[161]

To farm out these ongoing effects of British colonisation as Canadian or Australian stories, rather than British ones, is to deny their genesis in Britons' conviction that indigenous people had either to die out or have their 'colour bred out' (as one Australian Aboriginal Protector put it), by forcible assimilation. Distancing the fate of indigenous peoples from the story of Britain itself aids populist responses of denial and disavowal, but settler colonialism belongs to the story of Britain whether we like it or not.

Time and time again, in southern Africa, North America and Australasia, indigenous communities attempted to adapt to the 'civilization' of the British emigrants who were taking most of their land, telling them how to live on what remained, seizing their children, and restricting their mobility across landscapes that had been theirs for generations. They adopted and adapted Christianity, they wore European clothes, they adjusted their gender relationships so that women worked in the home (their own and those of settlers), while men did agricultural work; they ploughed the land left to them, they grew crops and they sold them to surrounding colonists. They accepted the management of well-meaning White missionaries, Protectors and station managers.

Time after time, in a pattern repeated across all of the settler colonies, they came under renewed pressure to vacate or sell what land remained to them, they succumbed to settler-elected governments who felt that their communal agriculture was unfair competition for White farmers; that their land should be sold off to settlers; that indigenous people were not suited to agriculture; that that they shouldn't live in towns either: that they should just disappear. Reserve lands, mission stations and protectorates — the small parcels of land to which indigenous peoples were confined by the late nineteenth century — were closed and sold off to White farmers; so-called 'half-castes' were ejected from those that remained and left to fend for themselves in settler society. These mixed-race people were not deemed aboriginal enough to live on reserves with their families, but neither were they White enough to qualify for basic citizenship rights in the surrounding colonial society. Denied the vote, they became in effect wards of the state, roundly condemned by White society for their resort to alcoholism and drug-dependency, for their vagrancy and for their criminality.[162]

Throughout the nineteenth century and well into the twentieth, Britons like Bannister at the humanitarian end of the spectrum, and Bowker at the genocidal end, engaged in their own rhetorical war, debating whether Black and indigenous people were capable of being civilised, and whether it was worthwhile making the effort. Most Britons who stayed at home to reap the rewards of Empire rather

India and the Settler Colonies

than risk their lives doing the dirty work of colonisation, would have decried Bowker's genocidal intent. But the point is that wherever they sat along the spectrum bookended by Bannister's and Bowker's positions, Britons were, almost without exception, racist. Without their sense of racial superiority, whether they saw it as bridgeable or regrettably permanent, there could be no legitimacy for an Empire constituted by White British dispossession of people of colour. This was why famous figures like Bartle Frere could articulate their anti-slavery and proclaim against colour prejudice whilst at the same time killing tens of thousands of Black South Africans so they could be absorbed in a confederated, British-run region

Chapter Ten

British Humanitarians: the 'Good' Imperialists

This is not to say that British colonists were evil monsters, however. People were as complex then as they are now. Over thirty years' research using the diaries, letters and journals of many British individuals, whose careers I have tracked across the Empire, I have come to empathise with a great many of them. Three figures with whom I identify stand out, for different reasons, and all three were implicated in the forms of either cultural or biological racism that marked the spectrum between Bannister and Bowker.

The least well known was Charles Lennox Stretch. He was a junior official on the eastern frontier of the Cape Colony during the 1830s, a time when some five thousand British settlers, most of whom had emigrated as part of a government-backed settlement scheme, were appropriating land belonging to the Xhosa people. They faced the consequences when an alliance of Xhosa chiefdoms launched an attack on their settlement in 1834 to reclaim grazing land that settlers were now carving up into private farms. This Sixth Frontier War ended in the amaXhosa's defeat, as would all nine of the frontier wars through which the Xhosa people sought to defend their land. In its aftermath, the colony annexed yet more Xhosa territory.

British Humanitarians: the 'Good Imperialists'

Stretch was one of the officials tasked with controlling the amaXhosa confined to reserves within that territory as the rest of it was parcelled out to the British settlers. He was complicit in the British invasion and theft of land, but he performed his duties with more compassion and humanity than any of the other British officials. Stretch felt empathy for the amaXhosa under his control. He allowed them to access the colony created on their former land for work or visits to kin who were working for settlers when other officials refused. He made their case for larger reserves to maintain the health of their cattle, when others argued the opposite. He sought punishment for settlers who attempted to force impoverished Xhosa into servitude on the farms that had once been theirs, while other officials constantly bemoaned the Xhosa's criminality as they raided those farms for food or revenge or accused them of laziness for refusing to work for their usurpers.

Ultimately Stretch's empathy for the Xhosa proved too much for other colonial frontier officials, who successfully lobbied the colonial administration to get him sacked. They claimed that his over-identification with the Xhosa was causing them to lose respect for the colonial administration as a whole.[163]

I can't help liking Stretch. But, at the same time, I must acknowledge that he, like his contemporaries, sincerely believed that British culture and civilization was better than the Xhosa's and that the British had a right to rule over them. He wanted that rule to be less avaricious and more sympathetic than many of his contemporaries though. Stretch wanted the outcome that today's apologists for the British Empire assume was its reality: British rule on behalf of the colonised. It was a stance, however, that put him at odds with most of his compatriots in the colony and with the general reality of that Empire.

Deny & Disavow

A second figure with whom I have developed a distanced rapport is Anna Gurney, a remarkable polymath from Norfolk. Gurney was part of a well-known Quaker family and worked alongside her cousin, Thomas Fowell Buxton. She was central to the humanitarian idea of empire articulated by Saxe Bannister, doing most of the work in drafting the Report of the Select Committee on Aborigines, which condemned British settler violence and called for a more Christian form of colonisation in 1837.

Disabled by polio in her childhood, Gurney was a wheelchair user best known today as either a pioneering scholar and translator of Anglo-Saxon English, or the friend of shipwrecked mariners, depending on your interest. She published the first translation of the Anglo-Saxon Chronicle into modern English in 1819, aged just 21, whilst 'striving to avoid the display of talents that might render her subject to the imputation of vanity or conceit' as a female author. Because of her gender, Gurney's publications in the journal of the Society of Antiquaries were anonymous until 1852.

Not only did she also purchase a Manby Life Saving Rocket which could be carried along the Norfolk shore to fire lifelines to distressed ships; she would ask to be carried down to the beach to direct rescue operations on the dangerous stretch of coast near her home and offer shelter and food to shipwrecked sailors. A speaker of Arabic, Danish, Dutch, French, German, ancient and modern Greek, Hebrew, Icelandic, Italian, Old English, Old Norse, Russian and Swedish, she was generally able to converse with the foreigners among them in their own languages.[164]

Gurney was described by her friend Elizabeth Whately as possessing 'an actual hunger and thirst for knowledge of all kinds, which knew no pause, and could never be satisfied'. She made it her mission to host visiting indigenous subjects

British Humanitarians: the 'Good Imperialists'

from Britain's colonies, most of them invited to England by her missionary friends. When the 'liberated African' Ajayi, who became Samuel Crowther, visited prior to being appointed the first African Bishop in Sierra Leone, Gurney learned Yoruba from him. She would go on to collaborate on a grammar of the Hausa language and work with the visiting African Baptist Augustus William Hanson on a translation of the scriptures into Accra.[165]

Gurney helped Buxton assemble and manage a network of missionary, philanthropic, governmental and settler correspondents which stretched around the world. Through these contacts they solicited and gathered information on the damage that British invasion was doing to Native American, Khoisan, Xhosa, Aboriginal, Pacific Islander, and Māori societies.

Gurney was a determined campaigner on behalf of Britain's Black imperial subjects. She firmly believed that their colonisation could be conducted in such a way that they could receive the benefits of Christianity, as she saw them, and British attainments in technology, science and medicine, without violent conquest and dispossession; that colonialism could be good for the colonised. The Aborigines Committee Report that she drafted was a scathing condemnation of the brutal dispossession of indigenous peoples on behalf of British settlers. Buxton referred to it as 'Aunt Anna (Gurney)'s report'; a document 'of vast importance to millions of mankind — and to the interests of the missionary cause'.[166]

Despite my affection for Gurney, I also cannot help recognising the limitations of the early Victorian evangelical preoccupations that restricted her and other humanitarians' ability to empathise with people of colour. To give an example, when the Aborigines Committee chaired by

Deny & Disavow

Buxton interviewed representatives of the Khoisan and Xhosa communities from the Cape Colony, they became diverted by the issue of whether these communities were being successfully converted to Christianity and learning to read and write from Bible study. They glossed rapidly over the representatives' complaints that conversion and education would be far easier if their land wasn't constantly being allocated to settlers backed by the British Army, their cattle herds declining, and their people starving as a result.

My third example of a British figure with whom I came to identify will be somewhat more controversial among those who know something of his record. George Arthur was the man who presided over the almost complete destruction of Tasmania's Aboriginal people.

During his tenure on the island colony, the dogged guerrilla resistance that Aboriginal groups put up against seizure of their land by British emigrants reached its denouement when Arthur declared martial law. The effect was to license settlers to form 'hunting' parties to track down and capture or kill, Aboriginal people. Caught between the British government policy that Tasmania (known as Van Diemen's Land at the time) should be opened to British settlement and his Christian concern for the Aboriginal people's fate, Arthur resorted to the assistance of a former builder from the East End of London, George Augustus Robinson.

Robinson offered to go around the island with Aboriginal guides and persuade the remainder of its inhabitants to surrender themselves to the care of the colonial government, rather than face total annihilation. His success enabled the remaining 200 (from an original population of between 3,000 and 15,000) to be taken to a purpose built, windswept settlement on Flinders Island, some 60 miles off the northeast coast of the main island. There they were

British Humanitarians: the 'Good Imperialists'

subjected to a regime of schooling and agricultural training intended to 'civilize' them. Without adequate sanitation or nutrition, the forty-eight of them who survived were finally allowed to return to Oyster Bay on the main island in 1847. Their deaths soon after meant that Tasmania's resurgent Aboriginal population today is descended primarily from Aboriginal women who escaped the same fate through cohabitation, often forced, with White sealers in the islands of the Bass Strait.

Prior to his arrival in the colony, Arthur had been governor of British Honduras, where his reputation was very different. Appalled by the British timber cutters' abuse of enslaved people, he brought in ameliorative codes to punish the worst excesses, and he unilaterally freed indigenous people who had been enslaved illegally. The British settlers there refused to work with him any longer and mobilised a campaign against him in the British press and parliament. He was recalled, becoming the darling of the anti-slavery lobby.

After Tasmania, Arthur was wracked with guilt about the effect of his decisions on the Aboriginal people. Indeed, he seems to have had a breakdown back in England. Part of his rehabilitation was ensuring a new policy for the protection of Aboriginal people on mainland Australia, in league with Buxton and Gurney. The protectorates of Aborigines that Arthur helped set up in the Port Phillip District (now Victoria), however, would go on later in the century to play a leading part in the adoption and fostering of the Stolen Generation.

Like many British colonial governors, Arthur was a man with a strong authoritarian streak. He would later have some of the American citizens who raided across Canada's border to support the 1837–8 rebellion executed, as a lesson to revolutionary democrats everywhere. But he also had a conscience and believed, like Gurney and Stretch (and, indeed, like some conservative commentators on empire today), in the possibility of a form of colonialism that could benefit colonised people as a whole. He shunned the British slave-owners of Honduras and was determinedly antislavery. Yet he also facilitated the most clear-cut example of genocide in the British Empire and set in train the process by which Aboriginal children would be removed from their families in a more systematic, bureaucratised fashion.

A tradition of British colonial humanitarianism, founded on people like Saxe Bannister, Gurney, Buxton, Stretch and Arthur, continued throughout the nineteenth and twentieth centuries. It was, to my mind, preferable to the exterminatory alternatives that Britons imagined at the time, given that so few seemed capable of respecting the differences or the independence of people of colour around the world. But even this more 'progressive' tradition was always marked by its racial paternalism.

Backlash: the invention of the proto-'woke'

By the 1850s, however, the term 'humanitarian' was becoming a recognisable stereotype in the hands of some of our most famous authors, and not a good one. 'Humanitarian' came into use to describe the naïve sentimentalist who believed in the ability of people of colour to become fully civilised and fully British, despite all the supposed evidence stacked against such an outcome. Today's accusations that those who highlight the violence of empire are 'anti-British' have antecedents in this mid-nineteenth century reaction against humanitarianism. It may not have been referred to at the time as a culture war but it did much to shape enduring divisions over race in Britain.

British Humanitarians: the 'Good Imperialists'

Thomas Carlyle and Charles Dickens were some of the key players in this forerunner of the culture war. They ridiculed people like Buxton and Gurney. In the wake of the abolition of slavery, Carlyle and Dickens thought that the antislavery philanthropists and missionary supporters had been proved wrong. The formerly enslaved had not diligently continued to work on the plantations, as philanthropists had promised. Instead, they had sought to reunite families torn apart when parents and children were sold to different owners. Choosing to live free of White planter control in the Jamaican highlands, freed slaves had deprived the planters of labour and caused sugar production to plummet.

When the 1846 Sugar Duties Act abolished the former slave owners' preferential rates on sugar imports, adding to their precipitous economic decline, Carlyle, fulminated against both the 'naïve' philanthropists and the free trade economists, who, between them, had helped free slaves into a state of wage labour while abandoning British planters. He argued that emancipation had condemned Black Jamaicans to idle pauperism, just as greater freedom had the Irish. The Irish, he argued, had been reduced to 'human swinery', a 'black howling Babel of superstitious savages' during the Famine. In a deliberately provocative article, which he boasted 'you will not, in the least like' entitled 'Occasional Discourse on the Negro Question', he described the freed slaves of Jamaica 'Sitting yonder, with their beautiful muzzles up to the ears in pumpkins, imbibing sweet pulps and juices; the grinder and incisor teeth ready for every new work; while the sugar crops rot round them, uncut, because labour cannot be hired'. [167]

And that was not all. Rather than listening to their missionaries and emulating the dour Christian services of Britons, freed slaves had shockingly blended Christianity with more vibrant forms of worship brought to the Caribbean on the slave ships from Africa. They had proved themselves not only incapable of diligent labour, but even of proper religious conversion.[168]

Carlyle and Dickens were convinced that Black and indigenous people had squandered the opportunity of freedom and the gift of civilisation that the British had offered them. They had proved the philanthropists not only misguided but dangerous. 'Humanitarians' were the 'wokes' of the Victorian era.

Dickens' *Bleak House* helped to invent the stereotype and fuelled antipathy to it. The book's character, Mrs Jellyby, is so obsessed with saving the souls of heathen Africans she has never met that she neglects her own children. Poor British children, like the road sweep Jo, die pitifully on the streets of London while the 'humanitarians' care only about distant savages who refuse to learn. The moral of the story was that, rather than continuing with their 'telescopic philanthropy', Britons should focus on the needs of White kith and kin at home. The parallels with the government's use of the Race Report to focus divisively on the needs of White working-class children, supposedly suffering because of Critical Race Theory's obsession with 'White privilege', is striking.

Despite the protests of liberal friends like John Stuart Mill, Carlyle's unabashed racism sharpened and articulated the British public's sense of disappointment in Africans' ability to become 'civilised'. Together with the stream of racial invective pouring into British homes from colonial newspapers extracted by the British press, in the private correspondence of settlers to their contacts at home, and in publications such as the *Memorials of the Settlers in the Eastern Cape*, it reinforced the notion that white Britons had a particular, if not unique, claim to that mantle of civilisation.

British Humanitarians: the 'Good Imperialists'

Carlyle and Dickens' ridicule of Britons who took an interest in the welfare of Black subjects overseas helped marginalise philanthropists' campaigns to accord them the same rights as White colonists during the later nineteenth century. As the franchise was extended to progressively poorer men in Britain in 1832, 1867 and 1884 (by which time two thirds of men, 18% of the population, could vote) it was race and gender, rather than class and gender, that continued to be the dominant forms of exclusion in the colonies. As British settlers overseas were enfranchised on more generous terms than those in Britain from the 1850s, armed rebellion in the Cape Colony led to a 'non-racial franchise' which allowed some Khoisan and Mfengu — former military allies of the settlers — to influence six constituencies. Such was the need to prevent more Africans voting, that the property bar was set to exclude the poorest Whites too. When more Africans qualified in the 1890s, it was lifted again.[169]

In the Australian colonies Aboriginal people were not necessarily explicitly barred from voting, but it was widely assumed that they would not. When 'Yellow Jimmy', a so-called 'half-caste', tried to vote in 1859, he was prosecuted for impersonating a White man. In New Zealand, Māori men could vote for four 'special' seats in 1867, their implicit right to register and vote on the common roll abolished. In proportion to their population share, they should have had fifteen seats. In Canada, First Nations men had to apply for exemption from their 'Indian' status, which meant giving up traditional ways, disassociating from kin and acquiring private property.[170] Far from dispensing democracy to its subjects, the British Empire withheld it on the grounds of race. In the Crown and settler colonies as in India, democracy was something for which independence movements had to fight against British rule.

The racialized nature of settler rule extended beyond the treatment of indigenous peoples, however, to include the organisation and manipulation of labour flows from other parts of the Empire and beyond. Beginning, as we have seen, in the 1830s, British colonial governments colluded with the Raj and with recruitment agents in China to establish large scale systems of indentured labour migration. These moved Asian people across great distances between British spheres of influence and the USA. Although they started off as the means by which enslaved labour would be replaced on plantations, by the 1850s settler governments were attuning these labour recruitment mechanisms to new kinds of labour demand.

Discoveries of valuable minerals, most notably gold, in British Columbia, California, Australia, New Zealand and the southern African Highveld, led to tremendous surges in immigration and urban development on a global scale.[171] White settler populations in these colonies needed Asian people's cheap labour in their mines, and yet, at the same time, they feared and resented their presence, anxious about a racial privilege that had only recently been won against indigenous people's resistance.

In the later nineteenth century politicians in both the USA and the British settler colonies cooperated in order to secure their respective 'white men's countries' against this self-induced and imaginary 'Asiatic menace'. What W B Du Bois called the Color Bar, long applied to African Americans, was reinforced across the Anglophone world. White people were accorded legal protection against non-white competition in education, housing and the job market.[172] Following American precedent, English language tests were often applied to limit access to these resources in the British settler colonies, without resorting to explicitly racist safeguards.

British Humanitarians: the 'Good Imperialists'

There is a tremendous irony in the continuity from the mid-nineteenth century's backlash against humanitarian sympathy with the colonised and today's backlash against Black Lives Matter and the 'woke'. Conservative culture warriors in pressure groups like Restore Trust and History Reclaimed now claim that emancipation from slavery and humanitarian concern for the welfare of colonised people were among Britain's greatest imperial achievements, distinguishing 'their' empire from others that were less progressive.

Chapter Eleven

There's No Moral Balance Sheet for the British Empire

The theologian and History Reclaimed co-founder Nigel Biggar leads a multidisciplinary project at Oxford designed to challenge the view that 'empire is ... unethical'. His project 'begs to differ'. Biggar has repeatedly explained why in the mainstream media, and he outlines the case in the introductory material on his project website.

On the one hand, Biggar admits, there were instances of violence such as the Tasmanian genocide and the Jallianwala Bagh (Amritsar) massacre, when Brigadier-general Dyer ordered troops to shoot at unarmed Indian protestors in 1919, killing at least 375 and up to 1,500 people. He also references the Irish Famine. But on the other hand, Biggar asserts, the British Empire 'suppressed the Atlantic and African slave trades after 1807, granted black Africans the vote in Cape Colony seventeen years before the United States granted it to African Americans and offered the only centre of armed resistance to European fascism between May 1940 and June 1941'.[173]

Putting these negative and positive features of empire in balance, he argues, will enable a 'historically intelligent Christian ethic of Empire'. Leaving aside all of the bits of

There's No Moral Balance Sheet for the British Empire

imperial history outlined above that Biggar chooses not to mention, including the recapture of liberated Africans, the subsequent denial of the vote to Black Africans in the Cape, and the fact that many imperial subjects of colour supported the fight against the Nazis in the belief that it would help them attain independence from Britain. One starting point for educating our children about the real British Empire is perhaps to take such a project — of finding its moral justification, and to explain why it is so problematic.

Biggar's suggestion of a moral balance sheet is the same argument that suggests Colston was morally defensible because he improved conditions for White people in Bristol while mass murdering and exploiting Black people to raise the funds. Ever since evangelical anti-slavery activists campaigned for Britain to abolish the transatlantic slave trade and humanitarians like Saxe Bannister took up their mantle, Britons have assured themselves that imperial overrule was compatible with the benign tutelage of other races and nations. Unlike the other European empires, Britons like Biggar tell themselves, theirs was an empire founded on humanitarian compassion for colonised subjects, and on the development of their societies.

The argument runs like this: while the Spanish, Portuguese, French, Belgians and Germans exploited and abused, the British Empire brought ideas of protection for lesser races and fostered their incremental development. With British tutelage colonised peoples could become, eventually, as competent, as knowledgeable, as 'civilised' as Britain itself. These platitudes have been repeated time and again — they are still at the heart of most popular representations of the British Empire. As we have seen, a version of them was voiced at the time too, by humanitarians. After emancipation they were marginalised by less paternalistic forms of racism.

Deny & Disavow

Even when apologists like Biggar encourage us to pay attention to Empire's costs as well as its benefits, these costs are imagined in terms of isolated and specific incidents of violence such as the 'Amritsar Massacre'. This focus on 'exceptional' occurrences elides the systematic nature of imperial violence, and of imperial racial discrimination. Not only were there the sixty 'small wars' in the late nineteenth century, but there was also a constant need to suppress dissent in conquered regions.

For my latest academic history, *Ruling the World*, we examined three years of British imperial governance in detail: 1838, 1857 and 1879. In those years alone, we estimate that around 1 million people of colour were killed by British forces and, at a conservative estimate, 2 million British subjects allowed to starve to death. The Victorian Empire's 'small wars' may have been small for Britain, but the killing of hundreds or a few thousands of people in any one indigenous community could be enough to shatter a relatively small society and deter further armed resistance. Furthermore, these wars were almost continual. In 1879 alone British forces conquered AmaXhosa, Griqua, Bapedi and AmaZulu in South Africa as well as invading Afghanistan for the second time. The use of scorched earth tactics against colonial foes like the Asante and Mahdist Sudanese was routine until it was deployed against White Boers. Then it caused outrage in Britain.

Such British violence was, and is, consistently disavowed in the iconography of colonial warfare. Think of the most famous paintings of Rorke's Drift and Isandlwana from the Anglo-Zulu War, and the sole (White) survivor of the first British invasion of Afghanistan reaching Jalalabad. All show redcoats under siege, defending barricades, forming squares, or escaping with their lives, after being assaulted by savage hordes. Wars of imperial aggression overseas

There's No Moral Balance Sheet for the British Empire

William Brydon was an assistant surgeon in the British East India Company Army during the First Anglo-Afghan War. He was believed to be the only member of an army of 4,500 men, plus 12,000 accompanying civilians, to reach safety in Jalalabad at the end of the long retreat from Kabul.

The Defence of Rorke's Drift, by Alphonse de Neuville (1880). The Battle of Rorke's Drift, also known as the Defence of Rorke's Drift, was an engagement in the Anglo-Zulu War in which a large force of Zulu warriors attacked a small British Garrison.

became the thin red line defending itself from onslaught in the public imagination at home.

Biggar's balance sheet tends to excuse Britain from that most often discussed injustice of empire — the slave trade and slave ownership — by the fact that it was Britain that pioneered abolition. By contrast, runs the same argument, the benefits that empire brought to the world are universal. Everyone should be grateful for the rule of law, the English language, modern education, railways and free trade: all things that Britain provided to usher in the modern age.

To remember empire in this way, as I hope to have shown in the previous chapters, is an act of incredible selectivity, if not wilful forgetting. Far from being of universal benefit, these 'positive' features of British rule were designed, in the first instance, to benefit British settlers, producers, traders and colonists. The partial inclusion of colonised peoples themselves in their benefits had to be hard won by those peoples in the face of racist laws and customs.

Black people generally weren't allowed to travel on the imperial railways on the same terms as White people. Gandhi, a man who was first impressed and loyal to, and later imprisoned by, the British when he fought for India's independence, received his political awakening when he was thrown out of a Whites only carriage on a South African railway. The shock was profound given that Gandhi had trained as a lawyer and been raised to believe that it was his capacity as a 'civilised' and educated man that defined his status, rather than his race.

Colonial government-run education systems varied hugely in time and place but were generally not extended to 'natives'. Their education was left to mission societies able to reach only a tiny proportion of them. As we have seen, where settler governments did make provision, the

There's No Moral Balance Sheet for the British Empire

Residential Schools of Canada and many of the institutions into which Aboriginal and so-called 'half-caste' children were forced in Australia were notoriously neglectful and abusive tools of forced assimilation, or cultural genocide. The mass schooling of Indians began after the Uprising and was intended to secure the compliance of the middle classes in the Raj's administration, but without engendering any aspiration to share power. Literacy rates tended to be higher in the princely states than in the areas directly governed by the Raj.

One of the first things that some indigenous elites did with the qualified education that Britons provided was challenge White peoples' entitlement to rule their countries, just as Salisbury had feared when he spoke of 'closing' the 'avenue' of education to them. The first generation of both the Indian and South African National Congresses, like Gandhi, asked only to be treated on the same terms as similarly educated Whites. It was when their pleas for equal treatment by cultural status were ignored and it was clear that the British would continue to treat them differentially by race, that their demands became more radical. Ultimately, they represented a challenge to the legitimacy of British rule itself and helped see to the end of the Empire in the mid-twentieth century.

The colonial 'rule of law', lauded similarly by apologists for imperial morality as if it was universally applied, as we have seen, also worked generally in favour of White settlers, elites and men. Even where explicitly racist legislation was avoided, proxies for race such as English language tests were used. These imposed different standards on 'native' populations without explicit racial discrimination and served to keep Asian people out of the British settler colonies unless their labour was required.

The wider adoption of English certainly facilitated more

global conversations and business transactions among elites, including Indian merchants and aristocrats. The long-established merchant class of Bombay for instance, did well out of access to Britain's global markets and credit supplies, and in partnership with British investors. But the inclusion of elites only served to heighten the exclusion of most non-English-speaking subjects and women from access to the credit and political capital that flowed through anglophone networks and was insufficient to assist famine victims.

Much the same could be said for free trade, which tended to enrich the colonial masters rather than most of their imperial subjects — let's not forget it was the argument for free trade which was used to force China to continue accepting opium imports against its will. Free trade was also enforced at the point of the gun in Latin America as it escaped Spanish and Portuguese rule to be dominated informally by British commercial interests.

That other much proclaimed 'benefit' of empire in Biggar's balance sheet — the gift of democracy — was, as we have seen, not a concept with which British elites were comfortable, or with which colonised peoples were familiar throughout most of the era of Britain's imperial rule. Rather, it was something hard won, largely by kicking the British out.

Perhaps most importantly of all, for people of colour around the world, the costs of empire were not restricted to the occasional episode of violent repression, nor even to structural injustices such as the slave trade, which Biggar and his allies are willing to put in their minimalist debit column. Rather, the costs of British colonialism for subjects of colour were systematic, routine and felt in everyday life. They included exclusion from power and privilege in their own lands coupled with humiliation at being made to pay deference to, and serve, White people, who assumed the right to govern them. While it is true that many colonised societies, like those of India, were deeply hierarchical before British rule, there was no distinction like that of the racial one upon which all colonists with White skins could rely under British rule.

Biggar and others' moral justifications for colonialism depend upon a rejection of the fact that it entrenched racial disparities. They tend to accord with the Commission on Race and Ethnic Disparities, arguing that any racial distinctions of empire (most of which they deny in the first place) were left behind when Britain decolonised; that allegations of structural racial discrimination today are a cynically motivated playing of the 'race card'.

Appreciating what happened to the idea of 'race' in the late imperial period and after empire is as important as understanding the ways in which British colonialism helped to create that idea during the late eighteenth and nineteenth centuries. We need to teach late- and post-colonial as well as colonial Britain if we are to assess the empire's effects.

Late Imperialism

Britain's retreat from Empire is often seen as beginning with the long-promised granting of independence to India (and Pakistan) in 1947. The seeds were planted earlier though. Although the Empire attained its greatest geographical extent with the addition of new territories after the First World War, their administration only added to the increasingly apparent inability to govern effectively across the world. The toll taken by the First World War, on Britain's population, its economy, its indebtedness and the loyalty of its White settler offshoots, was considerably higher than that of any of the preceding colonial campaigns. Promising the Holy Land to both wartime Arab allies and Jewish people in search of a state entangled British forces in an especially intractable Palestinian conflict that they could ill afford.

In March 2022, the then Education secretary Nadhim Zahawi argued that the 'benefits' of the British empire in the inter-war period should be taught to schoolchildren.[174] His choice of example, based on his own family background, is striking. He suggested instruction on the benefits that the colonial civil service brought to Iraq. The country can indeed serve as an instructive case study of late imperialism, although not necessarily in the way intended by the patriotic politician.

After the First World War, the new League of Nations allocated former colonies of the German and Ottoman empires to those of the victorious allies, to be governed on behalf of their subject peoples until such time as they were deemed ready for self-governance. They were called the mandated territories. The British government seized upon the opportunity to extend its influence across the oil rich Middle East, along a strategic belt between Suez and the Persian Gulf.

Britain had occupied the three Ottoman provinces of Mesopotamia during the war: Mosul in the north, Baghdad in the centre and Basra in the south. When British and Indian forces marched into Baghdad in 1917, they proclaimed themselves liberators rather than conquerors. T E Lawrence (of Arabia) suggested a form of governance on the model of the princely states in British India, but the British High Commissioner, Percy Cox, disagreed. Cox felt that 'the people of Mesopotamia had come to accept the fact of our occupation and were resigned to the prospect of a permanent British administration'. His successor, Col. Arnold Wilson, abolished what representative institutions the Ottoman Empire had installed and replaced Arab with

There's No Moral Balance Sheet for the British Empire

British officials. When the major powers met at the Paris Peace conference to establish the post-war global order and the League of Nations, Wilson refused permission for an Arab delegation to seek independence. Although the League of Nations insisted on the right of national self-determination within Europe, when it came to the colonies the interests of the local population were very much a secondary consideration. The strategic location and oil resources of the Middle East made it too attractive to allow for self-determination, as Zahawi's colleague, Kwasi Kwarteng, recognised in his well-researched *Ghosts of Empire*. Under the British occupation, the three Ottoman provinces were merged to create the modern state of Iraq, governed through the new civil service lauded by Zahawi.

However, the mandated government was effectively a military occupation. As Lawrence tried to explain, 'Things have been far worse than we have been told, our administration more bloody and inefficient than the public knows'. In 1919, the Kurds were the first to rebel, with British forces crushing their resistance. By June 1920, the occupying British forces were facing a much larger insurrection as disbanded ex-Ottoman soldiers, Islamists objecting to heathen governance and pro-independence Arab forces, both Sunni and Shia, combined to eject the British. A particular issue was the insensitivity of demanding a burial tax for Shias in the Wadi-us-Salaam Cemetery in Najaf. Facing 130,000 rebels the British army found itself embroiled in the largest British-led military campaign of the inter-war period. The commander in chief, General Haldane, cabled London that the 'rebellion has spread almost to Baghdad, where my position is by no means secure'.

The rebellion was gradually brought under control with methods similar to those of the Boer War. Mobile columns trapped rebels between blockhouses along railways and employed scorched earth tactics, burning villages, destroying food supplies and killing livestock, regardless of the impact on non-combatants. A new tactic was added, however, once War Secretary Winston Churchill authorised it. Rebel clusters were bombed from the air, with the British planning to use 'gas shells in quantity ... with excellent moral effect' among 100 tonnes of bombs. It is unclear whether they actually did so, although Churchill admitted, 'I do not understand this squeamishness about the use of gas. I am strongly in favour of using poison gas against uncivilised tribes ... [to] spread a lively terror'. Bomber Harris proclaimed that the Arabs and Kurds 'now know what real bombing means in casualties and damage. Within forty five minutes a full-size village can be practically wiped out and a third of its inhabitants killed or injured'.

By 1922, as the rebellion fizzled out, over four hundred British and Indian soldiers had been killed with rebel fatalities officially 8,450 but likely closer to 10,000 given the inability to count casualties of the bombs. Embarrassed by the cost and violence entailed in retaining direct rule, the British government installed its wartime Arab ally King Faisal, to govern the country with British interests in mind — an arrangement like that first proposed by Lawrence. Even after Iraqi independence in 1932, the British government insisted on retaining RAF bases with which to threaten continued bombing in the region. It did so to help its new client Iraqi regime suppress ongoing Kurdish resistance.

Few Britons know about it, but the rebellion against British rule in Iraq played a significant role in creating the Middle East as we know it today. It resulted in a pattern of Western-backed, authoritarian governments suppressing Arab nationalist movements. The prospects for democratic,

There's No Moral Balance Sheet for the British Empire

liberal states were squeezed between Western client states on the one hand and Islamic fundamentalist opposition to them on the other. Zahawi might believe that British schoolchildren should be persuaded to put the colonial civil service in Iraq in the credit column of an imagined imperial moral balance sheet. However, he seems to have overlooked its denial of sovereignty, its oppression, and its longer-term consequences for instability in the region.[175] The comparison with similar 'balance sheet' arguments in postwar Germany is instructive. As the noted historian Jürgen Zimmerer notes, mainstream German recognition of the need to address the crimes of the Holocaust came late, in the 1980s. For some forty years after World War II, most Germans sought solace for the previous generation's role in the Holocaust in exactly the kind of balance sheet approach that British imperial apologists use for the Empire today. They focused attention on Germans who opposed the Third Reich and pointed to 'achievements' like the construction of the autobahns and economic growth. The realisation that no 'credit column' could ever balance out the crimes against humanity in the 'debit' column came only later, and with the ensuing generation's refusal to countenance the excuses.[176]

The Empire Comes Home, or We are Here Because You Were There

If the moral lessons from teaching the latter stages of British imperialism are somewhat more complex than those envisaged by Biggar and the former Education Secretary, we also need to be more nuanced in the teaching of post-imperial British history. Britain emerged from World War II even more indebted to the USA, confronting better organised and supported nationalist movements objecting to White supremacy in many colonies, and a much-diminished power compared to the twin superpowers of the emerging Cold War. In the wake of World War II, the USA pressured British governments to abandon their Empire, opening it for further US investment, trade and influence, in return for American aid.[177]

The hubris of running the largest empire that the world had ever seen turned rapidly into anxiety.

When the British government decided to cut its losses in 1947 and withdraw from India hastily in the face of mounting antagonism, the Partition of the former Raj into India and Pakistan was a tragedy on a scale that few could have imagined. The division of Bengal and the Punjab between the two new countries based on district level Muslim or non-Muslim majorities displaced between 10 and 20 million people, creating an enormous refugee crisis. Up to two million people were killed in the ensuing communal violence.

While Britain left an India in turmoil, its attempts to preserve influence elsewhere generated some relatively smooth transitions to independence, such as in West Africa and the Gulf states. There, British 'protection' for recognised leaders who helped keep the Suez passage to India open and safe during the nineteenth century morphed into the UAE, Bahrain and Qatar, as a Labour government seeking to cut costs withdrew from empire East of Suez after 1968.[178]

Elsewhere though, the last-ditch defence of empire against mounting opposition took a bloody toll. Britain's various end-of-empire wars belie the myth that it gave up its empire voluntarily and peacefully. In Malaya, the British army fought a guerrilla war against Communist independence fighters between 1948 and 1960, using scorched earth policies, extrajudicial killings of villagers who supported

There's No Moral Balance Sheet for the British Empire

the rebels and the imprisonment in internment camps of some 400,000 to 500,000 civilians. The government's attempt, in league with the French and Israelis, to overturn President Nasser's nationalisation of the Suez Canal in 1956 was a particular marker of Britain's relative imperial decline amidst the rise of the new superpowers. American and Russian intervention forced a humiliating retreat.

In Kenya, British troops suppressing the Mau Mau revolt (1952–60) killed at least 11,000 rebels, executing over 1,000 once the fighting was over. Thirty-two European and twenty-six Asian civilians had been murdered by the rebels.[179] In Cyprus between 1955 and 1959 British troops fought against the EOKA Greek nationalist insurgency, paying compensation to thirty-three Cypriots who were tortured only in 2019. In Aden, between 1963 and 1967, the British tried to suppress Arab nationalist independence fighters with over 100 British deaths (including 17 civilians) and nearly 400 rebel deaths.

In 1959, the new Colonial secretary Iain Macleod was confronted by the simultaneous beating to death of eleven Mau Mau detainees at the Hola internment camp in Kenya and the killing of twenty Africans supporting independence in Nyasaland. This, he saw as a turning point: 'the decisive moment when it became clear to me that we could no longer continue with the old methods of government in Africa, and that meant inexorably a move towards African independence.'[180]

In 2011, the historian David Anderson, supporting a case for compensation by other Kenyan Mau Mau suspects who were tortured in British internment camps, helped to reveal that there was a 'migrated archive'. It consisted of thousands of official documents, many on the violence employed by British officials in attempts to hold on to the influence that empire accorded the British state. The Foreign Office had received these files from thirty-seven former colonies between the late 1940s and the 1970s and secreted them away from public view.[181]

While these wars of decolonisation were being fought overseas, politicians like Enoch Powell articulated and amplified the anxiety of the collapse of Empire at home. Added to the humiliation of events like Suez, was the reduction of the distance between White citizen and Black subject that imperial rule had manufactured and maintained for the last two hundred years. Powell created a tradition of White nativist objection to immigration into which today's conservative culture warriors have stepped.

In 1948 the British government offered its formerly colonised Black and brown subjects overseas citizenship and the right to live in the UK.[182] Between 1951 and 1971, after which new restrictions were placed on immigration from the former colonies, the proportion of foreign-born people in England and Wales (including many migrants from postwar Eastern Europe) rose from just over 4% to just over 6%. First among the large-scale migration from former colonies came the Windrush generation from the Caribbean and then much-needed workers and their families from what had been the Indian Raj.[183] They came to staff the new NHS, public transport and factories, and to play vital roles in providing local services.

The physical distancing that Empire had enabled most White Britons to sustain from British subjects of colour for over 300 years came to an end. The psychological distancing is taking longer. With the immigration of much larger numbers of Black and brown Britons to the place they had been taught to think of as the mother country, White Britons could no longer avoid or dismiss Black people's shared Britishness.

There's No Moral Balance Sheet for the British Empire

Many of the newly arrived Black Britons were like the Black intellectual Paul Gilroy's mother, a primary school head teacher who came to Britain from British Guiana, and who 'did not consider herself an immigrant: Like the rest of the Windrush generation, she was a citizen of the United Kingdom and colonies, moving from one part of the Empire to another'.[184] White Britons would now have to confront such people in their midst, either rejecting them or finding ways of allowing them to belong to a nationality that they had been brought up to consider White.[185]

Powell's infamous 'Rivers of Blood' speech, quoting a constituent who feared that 'in fifteen or twenty years' time the Black man will have the whip hand over the White man' in the UK, was delivered in April 1968, a month after I was born. I grew up in North London in a period when skinheads would hunt down Black and Asian people to beat and abuse, and when the use of the words N****r and P**i was routine. The youth leader of the National Front apparently attended my school. Since then, White Britons have been encouraged to unlearn their racism and legislation against its overt expression has strengthened, thanks in large part to the activism of Black people after incidents of racism such as the Bristol Bus Boycott (1963), the New Cross Fire (1981) and the murder of Stephen Lawrence (1993). We have come a long way.

Among ourselves though, in conspiratorial whispers and in social media posts, many White Britons continue to resent the imposition of such 'political correctness', or, more lately 'wokeness'. Most of my peers have never had the opportunity, motivation or need to confront the prejudices with which we were socialised, and persistent, structural racism is the result, whatever the Commission on Racial and Ethnic Disparity Report may say. The sheer scale of the

Deny & Disavow

Windrush scandal, in which Black Britons who arrived as children were suddenly informed that their presence in the UK was illegal, persecuted, and some of them 'repatriated' to countries they knew little or nothing of, indicates the persistence of this structural racism.[186] Culture war defences of the British Empire's legacies often pander to these prejudices.

Chapter Twelve

What are the British Empire's 'Legacies'?

How might those of us interested in history done with integrity get beyond an endlessly confrontational and unproductive repetition of simplistic binaries, of 'good' and 'bad' legacies and absurd moral balance sheets of the British Empire? I would suggest three main steps. First, we need to distinguish between legacies on the one hand and historical continuities and discontinuities on the other. Secondly, we should consider whether the idea of a legacy is substituting for nostalgia. And thirdly, we need to think beyond 'the British' as the only agents who mattered in the British Empire.

Continuities/Discontinuities

When commentators discuss legacies of the empire, what they are often referring to is not actually something that is handed down the generations, but rather the fiction of a moment frozen in time and preserved. A completely unrealistic concept given that change is continuous. It is the impossible and yet necessary job of the historian to study that change in all its complexity and variety. We can start by recognising that there is a distinction between the past and history, and then by acknowledging that history does not allow us clearly to distinguish legacies from any one frozen moment.

Hilary Mantel expressed the relationship between the past and history especially eloquently: 'Evidence is always partial. Facts are not truth, though they are part of it — information is not knowledge. And history is not the past — it is the method we have evolved of organising our ignorance of the past ... It's the plan of positions taken, when we stop the dance to slow them down. It's what's left in the sieve when the centuries have run through it — a few stones, scraps of writing, scraps of cloth. It's no more "the past" than a birth certificate is a birth, or a script is a performance, or a map is a journey.'[187]

If the past itself is unknowable except through such fragments, remnants and representations, its 'legacies' — the things that remain from an earlier time — are even more difficult to pin down. Traces of an empire that grew and contracted over 300 years, was pursued through business, governmental, philanthropic and emigrant settler projects, and that resulted from diverse interactions with multiple indigenous and other imperial actors, take various forms. To do history with integrity we need to differentiate between them, and to understand the ways that they change constantly.

Let us take public health in India as an example. On Twitter and elsewhere, members of History Reclaimed have seized upon advances in public health as a key beneficial legacy of British rule. The basis for these claims is notable scientific and medicinal advances against diseases such as smallpox and malaria, and the institution of public health programmes based upon them, mainly from the late nineteenth century. Subsequent improvements in public

What Are the British Empire's Legacies

health undoubtedly built upon both the scientific and practical lessons learned through these initiatives which took place under British rule.

However, Indians running Municipal, District and Village Boards were behind many of these initiatives, sometimes in the face of resistance from local British officials. As we have seen, British colonial governments generally cared little about the health of disenfranchised colonial subjects unless epidemic diseases threatened to spread to White colonial communities. The capacity of the colonial state was always limited and it had other priorities than public health.[188] A larger scale Indian public health service, funded by government, was spurred only by the threat of losing ground to the Quit India movement against British rule during World War II. Newly independent governments tended to invest far more in the health and welfare of their populations than had colonial governments. As Sunil Amrith notes, 'The claim to care for the welfare of the Indian people, in a way that no colonial government could do, was central to constructing the legitimacy of the post-colonial state'.[189]

Global health indices show far more drastic improvements after the demise not just of the British, but of all the European empires.[190] As the graph overleaf shows, infant mortality dropped precipitously in India only after independence in 1947. This correlation does not imply causation but it does suggest that the colonial government's interventions were a late and limited adjustment.

One could see all this as indicating simply that the post-1947 government of India took a positive if limited 'legacy' of British rule and made it more universally beneficial. Amrith, however, shows that things are more complicated even than this. 'The concerns of India's elite with racial purity and degeneration; the concern of social reformers

Deny & Disavow

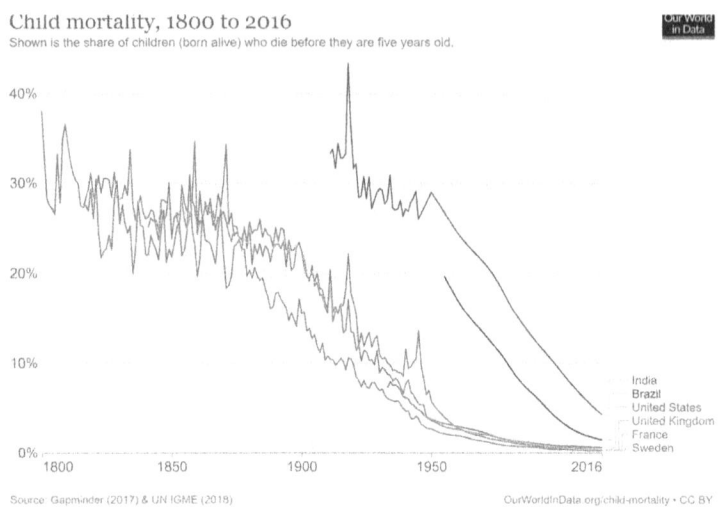

Child mortality, 1800 to 2016
Shown is the share of children (born alive) who die before they are five years old.

Source: Gapminder (2017) & UN IGME (2018)   OurWorldInData.org/child-mortality • CC BY

with the misery of India's villagers and the concern of modernists with using the state to transform society and economy — drawing on the most "advanced" models then available — melded in sometimes contradictory ways to shape the political culture of health in India'.

This blend of actors and motivations resulted in the world's most extensive malaria prevention campaign in the 1950s and 60s. It was funded more by American aid than British, and inspired by European, Soviet and New Zealand models of public health as well as British. The whole notion of distinguishing any straightforward British imperial 'legacy' of public health care in India becomes unsustainable in the light of this complex trajectory, and that is without even considering regional variations.

Can we credit 'the British' for public health improvements that they may have helped pioneer, but which occurred largely under an anti-colonial Indian movement? Can we separate 'British' scientific and medical advances in the first place from those of other collaborating scientists around

What Are the British Empire's Legacies

the world, and from the influence of Indians within the British administration who sometimes faced resistance from British officials? Can we say that it was British colonial precedents upon which the post-independence state built when it drew also upon public health interventions in the Soviet Union and elsewhere? What we can say is that when contemporary politics alone guides our approach to history, 'legacies' become simplified, distorted and conflated with finely wrought continuities and discontinuities.

Built and Institutional Legacies

The most tangible legacies from the imperial past are of the material kind: physical structures such as cities, schools, hospitals, railway stations, judicial and legislative buildings, roads, canals and bridges. Claimed by the defenders of colonialism as benefits bestowed by 'the British' and inherited by post-independence states, these were financed at least in part by British investors (albeit often with guarantees derived from taxing colonial subjects) and undertaken on British initiative. They were generally intended in the first instance to serve British military and business interests, though, and constructed by colonised labourers, who were often unpaid and coerced.

There may be general agreement about the continuing utility of many of these built legacies for post-colonial governments and populations. However, it all becomes more complicated once we start to examine their attribution to 'the British'. Can we credit British rule with the advent of more representative parliamentary institutions today when they inhabit a building such as the Union Building in Pretoria, designed by Hebert Baker for exclusively White legislators after the British government betrayed its promise to extend the non-racial franchise? Does such a building appear on the credit or debit side of imperial 'legacies' when it was put to service on behalf of the majority of the population only after British rule and the apartheid governments that succeeded it?

Many believe that the 'law and order' which inhabits colonial era judicial buildings is also a legacy of British rule, but of course some kind of law and order existed everywhere before British rule as well as after. What changed was its nature, most notably the groups it was designed to safeguard. Imperial apologists assert that British rule discriminated between different kinds of subjects less, was more impartial, less corruptible and less clientelist; that the neutrality and independence of the judiciary broke down only after the British left. Repression and everyday violence were characteristic of British rule though, as they are of any other form of discriminatory governance.

As we have seen, British law and order existed mainly to maintain White dominance in the colonies where British colonists dwelt. When the Colonial Office or India Office in London prescribed that colonial law be non-racial, that intent was generally undermined by local colonial interests. Since the demise of colonial regimes, of course law and order has often worked partially too, in favour of other minorities defined ethnically, regionally, by kinship or clientelism. In these instances, defenders of colonialism use phrases such as 'corruption'. They tend not to apply the term to equivalent British colonial practices that favoured White people.

James Fitzjames Stephen played a leading role in defining which of Britain's legal principles applied to India during the 1870s. He declared: 'If it be asked how the system works in practice, I can only say that it enables a handful of unsympathetic foreigners ... to rule justly and firmly about 200,000,000 persons of many races ...The Penal

What Are the British Empire's Legacies

Code, the Code of Criminal Procedure, and the institutions which they regulate, are somewhat grim presents for one people to make to another, and are little calculated to excite affection; but they are eminently well-calculated to protect peaceable men and to beat down wrongdoers, to extort respect, and to enforce obedience ... If, however, the authority of the Government is once materially relaxed, if the essential character of the enterprise is misunderstood and the delusion that it can be carried out by assemblies representing the opinions of the natives is admitted, nothing but anarchy, and ruin can be the result'.[191]

Enforcement of Stephen's law codes was entirely dependent on Indian policemen, record keepers and magistrates, employed in a vastly expanded Indian Civil Service and trained in new universities. But Indians were trusted neither to govern nor to make those laws.

Those approaching the imperial past with the justification of Britons in mind often deal in counterfactuals to evade such objections, arguing that if it were not for colonialism, neither the buildings themselves nor their current deployment for more democratic purposes would ever have developed in the colonies. The problem for historians who rely on sources relating to what actually happened rather than speculating about what might have happened, is evidencing those assertions. Democracy developed after decolonisation in some countries subject to British rule and not in others, and it also developed in countries that were never British colonies. None of the benefits of the world today compared to that in say 1900 are necessarily the result of colonial conquest. The simple answer, whether the institutions supporting democracy, railways or health care would have developed in former colonies without British rule, is and always will be 'who knows?'

Deny & Disavow

Nostalgia

If legacies of the past get artificially separated from continuities and discontinuities, they are also often mixed up with nostalgia: the longing for things to have remained the way that we imagine they were. The notion of a legacy preserves some notion of the past and makes it portable between generations, but most of the things that we want to preserve in this way never actually took the form we imagine. They are phantasms, dreams of what was and what might still be recovered.[192]

We may think that colonial nostalgia is a property only of conservatives, with their fondness for images of White memsahibs fanned by servants and District Officers telling the natives what to do. But nostalgia has a more flexible political utility. It can be both pro- and anti-colonial, as when Narendra Modi mobilises a sectarian vision of precolonial Hindu society against both Muslims and the Raj. When it comes to Hong Kong, nostalgia works for quite different agendas. For British conservatives it is seen as the prime example of a successful colony. Kwasi Kwarteng admits that 'the British Empire had nothing to do with liberal democracy', and shows how the last governor of Hong Kong, Chris Patten, introduced steps towards it only to frustrate the Chinese takeover. Nonetheless conservatives assert that the colony was governed with the consent of its subjects and with mutual prosperity in mind.

It is entirely understandable that a return to perceived colonial rule right now, for all its faults, would seem attractive not just to conservatives in the UK, but also to many dissident Chinese subjects in the former colony. But here too, nostalgia becomes conflated with legacy. Under British rule Hong Kong served as an imperial entrepot, creating wealth and opportunity for British and Chinese

What Are the British Empire's Legacies

business elites. However, the British elites insisted on racial exclusion. The expatriate White community excluded even elite Chinese from the most luxurious residential districts on the Peak and kept their social clubs racially exclusive. When they pressed for more democracy, it was for themselves alone and they intended to exclude those identified as Chinese from the franchise. Most Hong Kong subjects' well-being was left to Chinese and missionary charities until the 1950s, with British elites here, as elsewhere, concerned mainly about the risk of disease spreading to Whites. Yet these features of colonial rule are set aside as those subjected to active state repression in Hong Kong are inspired to resist by an alternative past.

More broadly too, nostalgia is a resource for those subjected to ever-evolving forms of oppression or poverty, including in the places that Britons once governed. Many Nigerians, for instance, express strong nostalgia for the days of British rule.[193] As David Lowenthal explained, 'Nostalgia reaffirms identities bruised by recent turmoil'. For many in Hong Kong the turmoil consists of the more vicious imposition of Chinese state authoritarianism. For conservatives in Britain, it is part of a more diffuse cultural change in which 'fundamental taken for granted convictions about man, woman, habits, manners, laws, society and God' are challenged by more inclusive values.[194]

Agency

Much of the problem with the discussion of imperial legacies is its continual re-centring of 'the British' as the only agents who matter in shaping them.

My first issue is with the word 'the' before 'British'. There never was any one British imperial project. As we have seen, how colonialism took root in each colony depended as much on tensions and debates among Britons as it did between Britons and other actors. Missionaries, philanthropists, businessmen, governing officials and settlers all had their own imperatives and favoured different kinds of relations with different groups of colonised people. Like the business elites in Hong Kong, certain of these groups predominated in particular colonies for particular periods.

In New Zealand, missionaries fought until 1840 to keep the Māori to themselves, since they saw them as potential converts who might be deterred by the unchristian behaviour of British traders and settlers. In West Africa in the late nineteenth century, it was palm oil and ivory traders who lay behind British attacks on African kingdoms, while in South Africa Rhodes faced opposition from liberal White politicians when he tried to centre the Cape Colony's policies around his mining business' demand for cheap African labour. We can no more assume a British consensus on colonialism, or a legacy of 'the' British, than we can consensus among Britons on any other political issue.

My second issue is to do with the focus on Britons, however attentive we are to their differences. What are thought of as legacies passed from one generation to the next are, as we have seen, continually reshaped, and not only by Britons. British colonists, like other historical actors, were entangled in relationships that they often dominated but never entirely controlled. These relationships were not only with other Britons pursuing different projects, but also with a diverse array of colonised peoples with their own varied agendas, and with those representing other empires. In our discussions of Empire, we need to challenge the sense of national exceptionalism that characterises the culture war.

In India British rule was entangled with the collapse of Mughal power, in Australasia and North America it was

What Are the British Empire's Legacies

spurred by French and other European rivalries; in central Asia and the Middle East some of the most dramatic (and disastrous) developments such as multiple invasions of Afghanistan were the result of fears of Russian expansion. By the same token, Britain's imperial decline was related to growing American and German influence and a Japanese insistence on modern imperialism being more than just a White European and North American project.

Aside from other empires, the pattern of British colonialism was inherently the result of interactions with colonised peoples themselves. The extent of their resistance, accommodation, adaptation, collaboration, and appropriation of British rule varied enormously across the different parts of the empire and over time. Whatever legacies we might imagine the British left behind are as much a product of their agency as that of 'the British', regardless of whether they are identified as positive or negative.

We might try to identify the legacies of the empire that all these actors forged by imagining it frozen in some snapshot taken at the moment of decolonisation in any particular colony. This would be Mantel's 'plan of positions taken, when we stop the dance to slow them down'. But however that frozen schema appeared, and however successful our attempts to characterise it, post-independence governments and populations were already repurposing it. Some of the features of those snapshots were allowed to fade into obscurity, some were sustained, extended and reconditioned for newly enfranchised citizens rather than subject peoples. Other features were continued, but in even more authoritarian guises. How can we possibly now distinguish between those features which can fairly be identified as legacies of Empire, to be blamed on, or credited to, 'the British', from those for which responsibility is more diffuse?

More to the point perhaps, was British conquest and racially discriminatory rule ever necessary for the dissemination of the medical, technological, and scientific advances often credited to it? I would suggest that the burden of proof is on those defending colonialism — a project that inevitably entails violence and conquest — to prove that they were, but I don't rate their chances.

Conclusion: Seven Apologists' Arguments

Any critique of the actions of the Britons who created and maintained the Empire evokes an impassioned response from those who are still invested in a White-centred 'national history' and the notion of a moral balance sheet that ignores race. When challenged with evidence of the empire's real nature, many of their arguments are predictable. I will end by responding to each of them briefly:

Argument 1

To highlight racism in the past is 'self-flagellating', and anti-British. It is motivated by the attempt to make White Britons today feel ashamed and guilty when they have done nothing wrong:

I do not want today's White Britons to feel ashamed or guilty. I do not blame us for what our ancestors did. I want us to adopt a more realistic understanding of the past, an important part of which was an imperial project of racial supremacy. We can be critical of our forebears and seek to improve upon their record of racism without beating ourselves up.[195]

Raising awareness of Empire's fundamental racism is not a sign, as Boris Johnson would have us believe, of 'cringing embarrassment about our history, about our traditions,

What Are the British Empire's Legacies

and about our culture' and it has nothing to do with 'self-recrimination and wetness'.[196] It is a step towards a more educated public, better equipped to recognise and combat the racism in our society that did not just appear one day from nowhere, but which has been part of a certain kind of British identity, bound up with Empire, for a very long time.

Argument 2

You shouldn't project today's values onto the past. You can't expect the Victorians to have had the same attitudes as us today:

Yes, I am projecting contemporary antiracist values onto a past where different values prevailed. However, this does not mean that I am misinterpreting that past. Understanding the racial thought of nineteenth century Britons, rather than denying that they ever had any, is key to understanding the past. It also better enables us to see the pernicious legacies today. My analysis of the past is based upon decades of archival work and immersion in the historical literature.

Those who insist on the moral 'balance' or even credit of the British Empire are also projecting today's values onto the past; it is just that they are doing so in wilful denial of its prevailing racial ideologies, in ignorance of the historiography, and in an attempt to resist antiracist endeavours in the present.

Argument 3

You criticise the British especially when they were no more flawed than any other people. Why focus on them rather than the violence and exploitation of the Nazis, Soviets, Mongols, Mughals, Persians, etc.

I do not consider the Britons who ran and profited

from the Empire anomalous or exceptional. They were not inhuman monsters. Through three decades of reading their despatches, letters, diaries and memoirs, I have developed empathy with many individuals among them. I am interested in how these people reconciled their roles in a system of violent racist exploitation with their sense of being humane. I think that therein lie lessons for us all.

I am also aware of all the arguments that seek to redirect attention from the British, often described as 'whataboutery'. Of all the arguments here, these are probably the most frequently heard. As David Olusoga has commented, 'Whenever I mention the British Empire in Africa, people will say "but what about the Belgians in the Congo?"... these aren't actual forms of dialogue, they are methods to stop a conversation happening; they are ways of silencing people.'[197]

Of course people other than Britons have traded, and continue to trade, in enslaved people; other empires of violent conquest have dominated recorded history, each of them committing atrocities; Belgian and German colonists committed crimes against humanity; many of the post-colonial governments that took over when the British left have fallen short for a complex array of reasons including corruption and denial of the sources of investment available to colonial regimes, etc. But my work and this book are about the British Empire. Is the fact that other empires were also discriminatory and violent a reason to deny and disavow what Britons demonstrably did? Should we censor that truth from our 'national story' just because it should appear in other national stories too? The 'whataboutery' argument is akin to criticising a researcher on cancer for not investigating tuberculosis.

Recent research on the psychology of denial is instructive

What Are the British Empire's Legacies

here. 'When presented with information about historical episodes in which their group has taken the role of perpetrator, individuals are likely to experience a sense of threat to their identity in the form of guilt or shame and may intuitively seek ways in which to avoid this threat. In such scenarios defensive reactions are often employed to negate the threat'. Alongside denial, the reaction that 'we might be bad, but at least we're not as bad as them' is a common one.

Experiments have shown that after people have been challenged with uncomfortable historical facts about the behaviour of the group they identify with, introducing the idea that other groups were just as bad can immediately restore their sense of pride. As the political scientist Joe Kendall notes, 'defensive reactions are not always instinctive and can easily be instrumentalised by political actors looking to gain from acrimonious culture wars'. Groups like History Reclaimed serve this purpose of finding and disseminating 'worse' examples of perpetration carried out by other groups. One of the side effects of the 'competitive innocence' they help to establish, however, is the loss of empathy with the victims of violent acts.[198] The notion that perpetrators in one's own national group must somehow have been justified in acting the way they did might well accompany the strategy.

Argument 4

You must not appreciate the benefits of being British/ living in Britain if you criticise your country like this:

I know that I am very privileged to have been born in Britain and that many other places are far worse to live in, including for people of colour. I appreciate that is why many migrants, including refugees and asylum seekers from conflict-torn and poverty-wracked countries, want to settle here. I believe that Britain will be an even better place to live if more of us stop denying our White supremacist past and accept the need for more inclusive ideas of national identity. The Euro 2020/21 England team provided a great example. I admired their taking the knee before every match in the tournament, even when our Home Secretary, astonishingly, condoned those who booed them. It was noteworthy that when player Tyrone Mings called out Priti Patel on Twitter, after the three Black players who failed to score penalties in the final were racially abused — 'You don't get to stoke the fire at the beginning of the tournament by labelling our anti-racism message as 'Gesture Politics' & then pretend to be disgusted when the very thing we're campaigning against, happens' — we began to see the first signs of moderate Conservative MPs speaking out against the populist culture warriors in their party. One senior party member said, 'I think there needs to be a serious realisation soon in government that people simply don't care about the culture war crap. They care about the cost of living, NHS and crime. They don't want to see us having fights with Marcus Rashford'.[199]

I agree that populist culture warriors' attempts to perpetuate division, to cast every political difference as a fundamental question of identity — as 'them versus us', 'woke' versus decent Britons — will not help Britain to be an even better place.

Argument 5

Your account is not balanced because you look only at the negative aspects of British imperialism and not the positive:

I have addressed the whole idea of balance sheet approaches above, and I have written about the genuine

What Are the British Empire's Legacies

humanitarian aspirations of many imperial Britons. Beyond this, yes, there were belated British efforts to invest in the 'development' of colonies on behalf of subjects of colour, mainly in the twentieth century when the Empire was under threat.[200] However the main intervention, the Colonial Development Act of 1929 'in practice did little to increase the flow [of money] from Britain. Little funding was provided and the legislation required that projects be formulated as much to create demand for British industry as to facilitate colonial development'.[201] There is a large literature on the ways in which colonial medicine and science were not simply gifted to colonised subjects by Britain, but, as we saw in the previous chapter, shaped through interaction between the British and the knowledge and demands of those they colonised.[202]

Argument 6

All lives should matter in history, not just Black lives:
I do not think that Black lives matter more than White lives. Of course, all lives matter, but it is Black lives that tend to have been disregarded throughout Britain's imperial history, while White lives have been privileged through colonialism and in our understanding of that history. Contemporary data, as indicated in the introduction, demonstrate that this disparity in the value of lives continues at an aggregate scale. Continuing to deny that is the problem.

Neither I nor the vast majority of Black Lives Matter supporters, as far as I am aware, want to privilege people of colour over White working-class people, or any other class of people, whatever populist politicians may have us believe. Acknowledging a divided past of White supremacy is the first step towards a shared, multi-racial future. Disavowing the racial divisions of the past is a recipe for division in the future. At the time of writing, it seems, that is just what the culture warriors would like.

Argument 7

You are driven by Critical Race Theory (CRT), a militant, Marxist-inspired, 'woke' doctrine that plagues current academia:

This argument is to be found in the right wing press and on History Reclaimed. Their purpose is to deflect from empirically substantiated observations of imperial violence and racism by associating them with Black Lives Matter-inspired political radicalism.

My work on the British Empire over the last 30 years has been conducted in complete ignorance of CRT. I became aware of it only after Twitter users 'accused' me of following its 'doctrine'. Curiosity then led me to read some of the literature seen as coming within this category. It is interesting stuff, mainly about the reasons why discrimination against African Americans continues within the country's judicial and penitentiary systems even after the Civil Rights movement secured legal equality. It has nothing to say about the British Empire and no historian of British colonialism of whom I am aware has cited it as an influence on their work. Imperial history writing emanates from different conceptual traditions and from first-hand archival research rather than from an American legal studies framework.

The tactic of aligning anything seen to be critical of British colonists with CRT originated among the USA's Trump-supporting extreme right wing. The 'Alt-Right' American commentator Christopher Rufo greatly facilitated my pinpointing of the source by boasting that he originated the tactic. It was he who first strove to make CRT 'toxic, as we put all the various cultural insanities under that brand category. The goal is to have the public read something crazy in the newspaper and immediately think "critical race theory".'[203] Since then, conservatives on both sides of the Atlantic and in Australia have complained incessantly that the CRT brainwashed 'woke' have polluted their children's education, their workplaces and their cultural institutions. As Michael Harriot puts it, the CRT label is nothing more than 'an attempt by the right to rebrand bigotry as a resistance movement'.[204]

.

Selective Further Reading

Empire as a whole

Christopher Bayly, *Imperial Meridian: The British Empire and the World 1780-1830*, Routledge, 1989.

John Darwin, *The Empire Project: The Rise and Fall of the British World System, 1830-1970*, Cambridge University Press, 2011.

Catherine Hall, Keith McClelland, Nicholas Draper, Katie Donington, and Rachel Lang, *Legacies of British Slave-ownership: Colonial Slavery and the Formation of Victorian Britain*, Cambridge University Press, 2014.

Alan Lester, Kate Boehme and Peter Mitchell, *Ruling the World: Freedom, Civilisation and Liberalism in the Nineteenth Century British Empire*, Cambridge University Press, 2021.

Philippa Levine, *The British Empire: Sunrise to Sunset*, Routledge 3rd edn, 2019.

John McKenzie, *Propaganda and Empire: The Manipulation of British Public Opinion, 1880-1960*, Manchester University Press, 1986.

The Caribbean

Hilary Beckles, *The First Black Slave Society: Britain's Barbados, 1636-1876*, University of the West Indies Press, 2016.

Trevor Burnard, *Mastery, Tyranny and Desire: Thomas*

Selective Further Reading

Thistlewood and His Slaves in the Anglo-Jamaican World, University of North Carolina Press, 2004.

Catherine Hall, *Civilising Subjects: Metropole and Colony in the English Imagination 1830-1867*, Verso, 2002.

Thomas C. Holt, *The Problem of Freedom, Race, Labor, and Politics in Jamaica and Britain, 1832-1938*, Johns Hopkins University Press, 1991.

Gad Heuman, *The Killing Time: The Morant Bay Rebellion in Jamaica*, University of Tennessee Press, 1994.

Eric Williams, *Capitalism and Slavery*, University of North Carolina Press, 1994.

India

H. V. Bowen, *The Business of Empire: The East India Company and Imperial Britain, 1756-1833*, Cambridge University Press, 2009.

William Dalrymple, *The Anarchy: The Relentless Rise of the East India Company*, Bloomsbury, 2021.

Pramod Nayar (ed.), *India 1857: The Great Uprising*, Penguin Books India, 2007.

Nick Robins, *The Corporation that Changed the World: How the East India Company Shaped the Modern Multinational*, Pluto Press, 2006.

Tirthankar Roy, *An Economic History of India, 1707-1857*, Routledge, 2nd ed., 2021.

Jon Wilson, *India Conquered: Britain's Raj and the Chaos of Empire*, Simon and Schuster, 2016

China

Julia Lovell, *The Opium War: Drugs, Dreams, and the Making of Modern China*, Picador, 2011.

Haijian Mao, *The Qing Empire and the Opium War: The Collapse of the Heavenly Dynasty*, Cambridge University Press, 2005.

J.Y. Wong, *Deadly Dreams: Opium and the Arrow War (1856-1860) in China*, Cambridge University Press, 1998.

The Settler Colonies

Tony Ballantyne, *Webs of Empire: Locating New Zealand's Past*, University of British Columbia Press, 2014.

Tracey Banivanua Mar and Penelope Edmonds (eds.), *Making Settler Colonial Space: Perspectives on Race, Place and Identity*, Palgrave, 2010.

Ann Curthoys and Jessie Mitchell, *Taking Liberty: Indigenous Rights and Settler Self-Government in Colonial Australia, 1830–1890*, Cambridge University Press, 2018.

Julie Evans, Patricia Grimshaw, David Philips and Shurlee Swain, *Equal Subjects, Unequal Rights: Indigenous Peoples in British Settler Colonies, 1830s-1910*, Manchester University Press, 2003.

John Laband, *Zulu Warriors: The Battle for the South African Frontier*, Yale University Press, 2014.

Zoë Laidlaw and Alan Lester (eds), *Indigenous Communities and Settler Colonialism: Land Holding, Loss and Survival in an Interconnected World*, Palgrave, 2015.

Selective Further Reading

Alan Lester, *Imperial Networks: Creating Identities in Nineteenth Century South Africa and Britain*, Routledge, 2001.

Adele Perry, *Colonial Relations: The Douglas-Connolly Family and the Nineteenth Century Imperial World*, Cambridge University Press, 2015.

References

1   Quoted by J. Darwin, The Empire Project: The Rise and Fall of the British World System, 1830–1970, Cambridge University Press, 2011, 268.

2   Joe Kendall, We Could Have Been Worse: Competitive Innocence and Defensive Memory Among Perpetrator Groups, unpublished manuscript.

3   https://www.ethnicity-facts-figures.service.gov.uk/

4   Zubaida Haque, Laia Becares and Nick Treloar, Over-Exposed and Under-Protected: The Devastating Impact of COVID-19 on Black and Minority Ethnic Communities in Great Britain, Runnymede Trust, Aug 2020

5   However, Colston might not have been quite as generous as Bristolians have assumed, since his major investment, the boys school, was founded mainly to supply sailors for his own ships. Sally Morgan, Memory and the merchants: Commemoration and civic identity, International Journal of Heritage Studies, 4, 2, 1998, 103– 113, DOI: 10.1080/13527259808722225; http://www.bris.

6   Madge Dresser, 'Colston Revisited', in Historians' Watch, June 27, 2020: https://www.historyworkshop.org. uk/colston-revisited/; https://www.bristolpost.

References

co.uk/news/ bristol-news/how-city-failed-remove-edward-4211771; James Watts, Edward Colston statue toppled: how Bristol came to see the slave trader as a hero and philanthropist: https://theconversation.com/edward-colston-statue- toppled-how-bristol-came-to-see-the-slave-trader-as-a- hero-and-philanthropist-140271

7 Quoted in James Walvin, A Short History of Slavery, Penguin, 2007, 48.

8 Walvin, Short History, 84.

9 https://www.bristolpost.co.uk/news/bristol-news/ how-city-failed-remove-edward-4211771

10 *Daily Telegraph*, 16 January 2021.

11 https://www.museumsassociation.org/museums-journal/news/2021/09/nadine-dorries-becomes-10th-culture-secretary-since-2010/

12 https://www.theartnewspaper.com/news/uk-culture-secretary-controversial-monuments

13 Ibid.

14 James Davison Hunter, Culture Wars: The Struggle To Control The Family, Art, Education, Law, And Politics In America, Basic Books, 1992.

15 Andrew Hartman, A War for the Soul of America: A History Of The Culture Wars, University of Chicago Press, 2019.

16 Zack Stanton, How the 'Culture War' Could Break Democracy: https://www.politico.com/news/magazine/2021/05/20/culture-war-politics-2021-democracy-analysis-489900

17 Jennifer Graham, 'The culture war will con-

tinue to rage in 2021': https://www.deseret.com/ indepth/2021/1/3/22159761/cancel-culture-wars-abortion-media-partisan-divide-morality-trust-american- community

18   Stanton, https://www.politico.com/news/magazine/2021/05/20/culture-war-politics-2021-democracy-analysis-489900

19   Ibid.

20   https://www.independent.co.uk/property/interiors/ carefully-edited-andrew-neil-s-french-retreat-858077.html

21   Jennifer Graham, 'The culture war will continue to rage in 2021': https://www.deseret.com/indepth/2021/1/3/22159761/cancel-culture-wars-abortion-media-partisan-divide-morality-trust-american- community

22   The Guardian, 4 Dec 2021.

23   https://www.newyorker.com/news/annals-of-inquiry/how-a-conservative-activist-invented-the-conflict-over-critical-race-theory. For an example of how the right wing press has construed the 'pernicious doctrine', see https://www.telegraph.co.uk/news/2020/10/01/beware-critical-race-theory-divisive-ideology-infiltrating/. To read some critical race theory itself and gain a sense of how it is distorted beyond recognition by this backlash, see Kimberlé Crenshaw, Neil Gotanda, Gary Peller and Kendall Thomas (eds) Critical Race Theory: The Key Writings that Formed a Movement, The New Press, 1995.

24   https://www.theguardian.com/commentisfree/2020/ jun/20/the-far-left-origins-of-no-10s-desperate-attack-on- all-things-woke

References

25 . See the crowd sourced map of other statues with links to slavery and colonialism: https://www.toppletheracists.org/

26 https://www.guysandstthomas.nhs.uk/news-and- events/2020-news/june/200611-joint-statement-on-statues. aspx

27 https://www.maryseacoletrust.org.uk/mary-seacole- statue/

28 Avril Nanton and Jody Burton, Black London: History, Art & Culture in Over 120 Places, Inkspire, 2021. See https://www.theguardian.com/world/2021/jun/20/from- tudor-courts-to-blm-a-new-book-brings-londons-Black- history-to-life?CMP=Share_iOSApp_Other

29 Elizabeth Kolsky, Colonial Justice in British India. White Violence and the Rule of Law, Cambridge University Press, 2010, 16.

30 Walvin, A Short History, 134.

31 Alan Lester, Kate Boehme and Peter Mitchell, Ruling the World: Freedom, Civilisation and Liberalism in the Nineteenth Century British Empire, Cambridge University Press, 2021

32 https://www.theguardian.com/commentisfree/2020/jun./11/robert-clive-statue-Whitehall-british-imperial

33 Bowen, H. Clive, Robert, first Baron Clive of Plassey (1725–1774), army officer in the East India Company and administrator in India. Oxford Dictionary of National Biography. Retrieved Jun. 2021, from https://www.oxforddnb.com/view/10.1093/

ref:odnb/9780198614128.001.0001/odnb-9780198614128-e-5697.

34   Margot Finn and Kate Smith (eds) The East India Company at Home, UCL Press, 2018; https://blogs.ucl.ac.uk/eicah/

35   https://www.nationaltrust.org.uk/visit/wales/powis-castle-and-garden/the-clive-museum-collection-at-powis-castle

36   Bowen, H. Clive, Robert, first Baron Clive of Plassey (1725–1774), army officer in the East India Company and administrator in India. Oxford Dictionary of National Biography. Retrieved 24 Jun. 2021, from https://www.oxforddnb.com/view/10.1093/ref:odnb/9780198614128.001.0001/odnb-9780198614128-e-5697.

37   William Dalrymple, The Anarchy: The Relentless Rise of the East India Company, Bloomsbury, 2019, 234-5.

38   Richard Goebelt, 'The memory of Lord Clive in Britain and beyond: Imperial hero and villain', in Dominik Geppert and Frank Lorenz Müller (eds), Sites of imperial memory: Commemorating colonial rule in the nineteenth and twentieth centuries, Manchester University Press, 2016.

39   Nick Robins, The Corporation that Changed the World; @removeclive

40   Hansard, 10 July 1833 vol 19 cc479-550.

41   Martin Daunton, Tax Transfers: Britain and its Empire, 1848 1914. In: Nehring H., Schui F. (eds) Global Debates about Taxation. Palgrave Macmillan, 2007: https://doi.org/10.1057/9780230625518_8

References

42   S. Ahmed Khan, The Causes of the Indian Revolt, Medical Hall Press, 1873, 14.

43   D. Howlett, 'Ramsay, James Andrew Broun, first marquess of Dalhousie (1812–1860), governor-general of India' Oxford Dictionary of National Biography, 2011. Retrieved 15 Jul. 2019, from https://www.oxforddnb.com/

44   E. Stokes, The English Utilitarians and India, Oxford University Press, Delhi, 1989, 250.

45   Manchester's cloth exporters had agitated for a rail line from Bombay inland to Thane so that they could access cheaper Indian cotton in 1846, but the railway opened only in 1853. The first train to navigate its steep and difficult route was watched by millions of Indian subjects. A line constructed in Bengal was also driven by British commercial interests, to bring coal from Raniganj to the Hooghly River near Calcutta. Here, the first transit had been delayed until 1855 because an expensive clerical error in Britain led to the locomotives being sent to Australia instead of Calcutta: C. Wolmar, Blood, Iron and Gold: How the Railways Transformed the World, Atlantic Books, 2009.

46   Headrick The Tools of Empire: Technology and European Imperialism in the Nineteenth Century, Oxford University Press, 1981, 180.

47   It is estimated that 25,000 Indian labourers, referred to dismissively as 'coolies' by the British engineers, died in the construction of the Ghat inclines alone: A. Burton, On the Rails: Two Centuries of Railways, Aurum, 2004, 135.

48   D. Howlett, "Ramsay, James Andrew Broun, First Marquess of Dalhousie (1812–1860), Governor-General of India", Oxford Dictionary of National Biography, 2011.

Retrieved 3 Jun. 2019, from https://www.oxforddnb.com/view/10.1093/ref:odnb/9780198614128.001.0001/odnb-9780198614128-e-23088.

49   Ibid.

50   Rango Bapujee, Rajah of Sattara: A Letter to the Right Hon. J. C. Herries, M.P., President of the Board of Control, G. Norman, 1852: http://www.csas.ed.ac.uk/mutiny/Part1Texts.html

51   Howlett, Ramsay, James Andrew Broun, First Marquess of Dalhousie.

52   Roy, An Economic History of India, 10.

53   J. Wilson, India Conquered: Britain's Raj and the Chaos of Empire, Simon and Schuster, 2016, 235.

54   Ibid.

55   Ibid 230.

56   C. Bates, Commemorating 1857, from C. Bates, Subalterns and Raj: South Asia since 1600, Routledge 2007, http://www.csas.ed.ac.uk/mutiny/history.html. Retrieved 17 Jun. 2019.

57   Wilson, India Conquered, 240.

58   When Burma was first being conquered in 1824, the issue of passage across the Bay of Bengal had played a part in prompting sepoys to mutiny at the Company's garrison at Barrackpoor near Calcutta. One hundred and eighty of them had been shot dead in a panicked response from British officers that was later condemned in Britain.

59   Khan, The Causes, 14.

60   P. Scheckner, An Anthology of Chartist poetry:

References

poetry of the British working class, 1830s–1850s, Fairleigh Dickinson University Press, 1989, 53.

61   Forty One Years in India — From Subaltern to Commander-in-Chief — Lord Roberts of Kandahar — www.gutenberg.org

62   Hao Gao, Creating the Opium War: British Imperial Attitudes Towards China, 1792–1840, Manchester University Press, 2020; Mao Haijian, The Qing Empire and the Opium War: The Collapse of the Heavenly Dynasty, trans. Joseph Lawson, Cambridge University Press, 2005.

63   J. Wong, Deadly Dreams: Opium and the Arrow War (1856–1860) in China, Cambridge University Press, 1998.

64   Hansard, 3 February–21 March 1857.

65   Gao, Creating the Opium War; Haijian, The Qing Empire and the Opium War; Reynolds's Newspaper 22 March 1857.

66   D. C. Boulger, The Life of Gordon, T. F. Unwin, 1897, 45–46

67   Quoted in Lester, Boehme and Mitchell, Ruling the World, 297.

68   https://www.africavenir.org/nc/news-details/article/kwame-opoku-when-will-britain-return-looted-ghanaian-artefacts-a-history-of-british-looting-of-mor.html. Thanks to Mary-Ann Middlekoop for information on this.

69   See, for example, Dan Hicks, The British Museums: The Benin Bronzes, Colonial Violence and Cultural Restitution, Pluto Press, 2020.

70   https://www.military-history.org/books/small-wars-military-classics.htm; Charles Edward Callwell, Small Wars: Their Principles and Practice, Book Jungle, reproduced 2009.

71   Richard Huzzey, Freedom Burning: Anti-slavery and Empire in Victorian Britain, Cornell University Press, 2012, p. 133. See also Padraic X. Scanlan, Slave Empire: How Slavery Built Modern Britain, Robinson, 2020.

72   R. J. Gavin, 'The Bartle Frere Mission to Zanzibar, 1873', The Historical Journal, 5, 2, 1962.

73   Fergus Nicoll, The Sword of the Prophet: The Mahdi of Sudan and the Death of General Gordon, Sutton, 2004.

74   Paul Maylam, The Cult of Rhodes: Remembering an Imperialist in Africa, David Philip, 2005, 11.

75   Iain McCallum, Blood Brothers: Hiram and Hudson Maxim—Pioneers of Modern Warfare, Chatham Publishing, 1999, 67.

76   A. R. Dilley, 'The Economics of Empire', in Sarah Stockwell ed, The British Empire: Themes and Perspectives, Blackwell, 2008, 112.

77   Rhodes believed that a shared Saxon heritage meant that Germans could unite with the Anglo-Saxon British and Americans to dominate the world, but after the First World War, German eligibility for the scheme was removed. It proved much harder to remove the requirement that the scholarships were for men only. Women were only admitted in the 1970s.

78   https://www.theguardian.com/education/2021/may/19/cecil-rhodes-statue-at-oxford-college-should-go-

References

says-independent-report?CMP=Share_iOSApp_Other. Cecil Rhodes statue will not be removed by Oxford College: https://www.bbc.co.uk/news/uk-england-oxfordshire-57175057

79 Telegraph, 7 Feb 2021.

80 Malam, The Cult of Rhodes, 4. For a review of Biggar's recent book-length defence of empire, Colonialism: A Moral Reckoning, see https://bellacaledonia.org.uk/2023/03/07/the-british-empire-rehabilitated/#comment-626454

81 https://thecritic.co.uk/violence-against-history/

82 Trevor Phillips has helped set up a group called History Matters, backed by the centre-right think tank Policy Exchange, which seeks to list statues and other aspects of material culture supposedly 'under threat' from historical reinterpretation. He included a false statement in his glowing review of Nigel Biggar's book Colonialism, that a group of Biggar's Oxford colleagues had called for Biggar's new centre to be shut down. They had simply expressed their disagreement with his approach to empire, and the newspaper that carried the review was forced by the Independent Press Standards Office to issue a correction (Sunday Times, 26 Feb 2023). See Margot C. Finn, Presidential Address: Material Turns in British History: IV. Empire in India, Cancel Cultures and the Country House, Transactions of the Royal Historical Society, XXXI, 1-22. For my debate with Robert Tombs, see https://historyreclaimed.co.uk/ debating-the-british-empire/83 https://www.theartnewspaper.com/news/uk-culture-secretary-controversial-monuments

84 https://www.thecommonsensegroup.com/wp-content/uploads/2021/05/Common-Sense.pdf

85   Hayes was the man to whom Suella Braverman, in defiance of the ministerial code, sent emails containing proposed immigration restriction measures. It led to her temporary resignation under Truss before her re-appointment as Home Secretary by Sunak.

86   https://obr.uk/forecasts-in-depth/the-economy-forecast/brexit-analysis/#assumptions

87   Peter Mitchell, Imperial Nostalgia: How the British Conquered Themselves, Manchester University Press, 2021, 16

88   https://www.bbc.co.uk/news/education-55893706

89   https://www.ethnicity-facts-figures.service.gov.uk/

90   https://www.Blacklivesmatter.uk

91   https://news.sky.com/story/tory-leadership-race-rishi-sunak-vows-to-stop-woke-nonsense-and-left-wing-agitators-in-latest-pledge-12661643;

92   https://www.independent.co.uk/news/uk/politics/Black-lives-matter-protests-uk-boris-johnson-slavery-statues-george- floyd-a9563541.html

93   The Independent, 31 March 2021.

94   https://committees.parliament.uk/publications/6364/ documents/69838/default/

95   https://www.gov.uk/government/publications/the-report-   of-the-commission-on-race-and-ethnic-disparities

96   Quoted Eric Stokes, The English Utilitarians and India, Oxford University Press, 1989, 297–8.

97   For common defences of slavery see Michael

References

Taylor, The Interest: How the British Establishment Resisted the Abolition of Slavery, Vintage, 2020.

98 Kim Wagner, Amritsar 1919: An Empire of Fear and the Making of a Massacre, Yale University Press, 2019; Sathnam Sanghera, https://www.channel4.com/programmes/the-massacre- that-shook-the-empire; Alan Lester, https://theconversation. com/britain-should-stop-trying-to-pretend-that-its-empire-was- benevolent-59298

99 Sathnam Sanghera, Empireland: How Imperialism has Shaped Modern Britain, Viking, 2021, 208.

100 See for example https://www.runnymedetrust.org/ sewell and https://www.sussex.ac.uk/webteam/gateway/file. php?name=cie-views-on-the-sewell-report.pdf&site=320

101 https://unherd.com/thepost/why-the-race-equalities- report-is-so-subversive/?=frpo

102 https://www.chanel4.com/news/the-report-part-1-race- and-the-system

103 https://www.runnymedetrust.org/sewell

104 https://bylinetimes.com/2021/04/09/race-report-sewell- commission-couldnt-find-something-it-wasnt-looking-for/

105 Portes concludes, 'In 35 years of both producing and consuming government reports, I don't think I have ever seen one where the evidence and analysis has been so comprehensively discredited so quickly and completely'. In an unusual intervention, the United Nations was moved to label the Race Report an 'attempt to normalise White supremacy': https://www.runnymedetrust.org/ sewell

106 https://committees.parliament.uk/publications/6364/documents/69838/default/.

107 Stephanie Barczewski, Country Houses and the British Empire, 1700–1930, Manchester University Press, 2016.

108 https://bylinetimes.com/2022/10/27/the-right wing-bid-to-capture-the-national-trust-exposed/

109 Centenary Inaugural Lecture — Professor Corinne Fowler, Rewriting History? Heritage, Rurality and Empire. The same result ensued later in 2021 when the Common Sense group appealed to the Charities regulator over the Barnado's charity's use of the term 'white privilege'. https://www.youtube.com/watch?v=oIUljLIZZ_g

110 https://www.thepinknews.com/2021/10/15/national-trust-christian-voice-stephen-green/

111 https://www.thirdsector.co.uk/national-trust-hits-back-paid-for-campaign-influence-its-governance/governance/article/1796749

112 Telegraph, 20 May 2021

113 https://www.nationaltrust.org.uk/features/addressing-the-histories-of-slavery-and-colonialism-at-the-national-trust

114 https://twitter.com/corinne_fowler/status/1404819434087358470

115 Telegraph, 22 Nov 2020.

116 The Times 17 May 2021.

117 https://www.theguardian.com/

References

commentisfree/2022/may/12/hate-mail-death-threats-culture-war-matthew-katzman-cancelling-queen

118   Mail on Sunday 13 June 21; The Sunday Telegraph, 13 June 21.

119   https://www.theguardian.com/world/2021/jun/15/samuel-kasumu-boris-johnson-race-adviser-tories- culture-wars?CMP=Share_iOSApp_Other

120   The Guardian 12 June 2021.

121   Björn Weiler, Reclaiming History, https://bkw488.wixsite.com/highmedievalpast/post/reclaiming-history

122   https://www.telegraph.co.uk/news/2020/06/20/academics-fear-mobbed-stand-british-empire-oxford-scholar-says/

123   https://www.dailymail.co.uk/news/article-9153499/ Academic-says-GARDENING-roots-racial-injustice.html

124   The Times 12 May 2021.

125   Alan F C Ryder, Benin and the Europeans 1485–1897, Longmans, 1969; Hicks, The Brutish Museums.

126   https://historyreclaimed.co.uk/where-are-nigerias-benin-bronzes/; https://thecritic.co.uk/whites-and-wrongs/

127   Evo Ekpo, The Dialects of Definitions: "Massacre" and "sack" in the history of the Punitive Expedition, African Arts, 30, 3, Summer 1997, 34-5; James D. Graham, The Slave Trade, Depopulation and Human Sacrifice in Benin History: The general approach, Cahiers d'Études Africaines , 5, 18, 1965, 317-334.

128   https://adjaye.com/work/edo-museum-of-west-african-art/…

129   https://historyreclaimed.co.uk/the-costs-of-abolition/

130   For specialist accounts of the British antislavery measures see Maeve Ryan, Humanitarian Governance and the British Anti-Slavery World System, Yale University Press, 2022 and Bronwen Everill, Not Made By Slaves: Ethical Capitalism in the Age of Abolition, Harvard University Press, 2020 and Abolition and Empire in Sierra Leone and Liberia, Cambridge Series in Imperial and Post-colonial Studies, Palgrave Macmillan, 2013.

131   https://historyreclaimed.co.uk/the-woke-onslaught-is-a-war-on-the-west-itself/

132   https://www.telegraph.co.uk/news/2022/12/28/bbc-guilty-rewriting-british-history-promote-woke-agenda-biased/; https://www.spectator.co.uk/article/the-bbc-is-failing-impartiality-with-its-history-documentaries/

133   https://twitter.com/aljhlester/

134.   Richard J. Evans, Lying About Hitler: History, Holocaust and the David Irving Trial, Basic Books, 2002, 2.

135.   Evans, Lying About Hitler, 42, quoting Robert Harris.

136.   https://www.ucl.ac.uk/lbs/search/. For examples from Devon, see https://www.ucl.ac.uk/lbs/media-new/pdfs/devonandslaveownership.pdf

137.   https://blogs.ucl.ac.uk/eicah/

References

138. https://www.theguardian.com/media/2020/nov/13/ daily-mail-pays-25000-to-professor-it-falsely-accused-of- inciting-race-war-priyamvada-gopal-fake-tweets

139. https://www.dailymail.co.uk/news/article-9153499/ Academic-says-GARDENING-roots-racial-injustice.html

140. https://lbsatucl.wordpress.com/2021/02/17/culture-wars-in-country-houses-what-the-national-trust- controversy-tells-us-about-british-history-today/

141. https://www.dailymail.co.uk/news/article-9153499/ Academic-says-GARDENING-roots-racial-injustice.html; Corinne Fowler, Green Unpleasant Land: Creative Responses to Britain's Colonial Connections, Peepal Tree Press, 2020. The phrase 'convivial culture' is from Paul Gilroy, as Fowler acknowledges.

142. This section is adapted from an article written for BBC History Magazine, April 2021.

143. See Stuart Macintyre and Anna Clark, The History Wars, Melbourne University Press, 2013; Robert Manne, Whitewash: On Keith Windschuttle's Fabrication of Aboriginal History, Black Inc. 2003; Doug Munro, History Wars: The Peter Ryan — Manning Clark Controversy, ANU Press 2021https:// press.anu.edu.au/publications/history-wars and the map of British settler's massacres of Aboriginal people in Australia at https://c21ch.newcastle.edu.au/colonialmassacres/map.php

144. https://www.historyworkshop.org.uk/slavery-and-australian-colonisation/. See also https://australian-

legacies-slavery.org/; https://www.historyworkshop.org. uk/Black-lives-still-dont-matter-here/; Emma Christopher, 'An Illegitimate Offspring: South Sea Islanders, Queensland Sugar, and the Heirs of the British Atlantic Slave Complex', History Workshop Journal, 90, 2020, 233–252.

145. Aaron Graham, Slavery, Banks and the Ambivalent Legacies of Compensation in South Africa, Mauritius and the Caribbean, Journal of Southern African Studies, 2021,DOI: 10.1080/03057070.2021.1899465

146. https://imperialglobalexeter.com/2019/07/11/how-the-century-of-humiliation-influences-chinas-ambitions-today/

147. Amartya Sen, Illusions of empire: on what British rule really did for India, The Guardian, 29 June 2021

148. D. E. Haynes, Rhetoric and Ritual in Colonial India: The Shaping of a Public Culture in Surat City, 1852-1928, Oxford University Press, 1992, 97; C. A. Bayly, Recovering Liberties: Indian Thought in the Age of Liberalism and Empire, Cambridge University Press, 2012.

149. P. Smith, 'Cecil, Robert Arthur Talbot Gascoyne-, third marquess of Salisbury (1830–1903), prime minister, Oxford Dictionary of National Biography, 2011, retrieved 14 March 2023.

28 Oct. 2019, from https://www.oxforddnb.com/view/10.1093/ref:odnb/9780198614128.001.0001/odnb-9780198614128-e-32339

150. Government of the Raj 1858–1914: Parliament.uk

References

151. https://amp.theguardian.com/uk-news/2021/apr/22/scandal-of-unequal-commemoration-of-uks-ww1-dead-known-about

152. Quoted in Sen, Illusions of empire

153. Roy, An Economic History, 12, 10.

154. Gurminder Bhambra, Focus: Accounting for British History https://archive.discoversociety.org/2020/07/01/ focus-accounting-for-british-history/

155. Sen, Illusions of empire.

156. Select Committee on Aborigines (British Settlements) Report, 1837, quoted in, Alan Lester, Imperial Networks: Creating Identities in Nineteenth Century South Africa and Britain, Routledge, 2001, 112.

157. Ibid., 44.

158. Quoted in Lester, Imperial Networks, 64.

159. https://nctr.ca/records/reports/

160. Glenbow Museum, M-1356-6, 28, 65, 70 Calgary Indian Missions Medical Reports; The former Indian Agent George Gooderham's history of the residential schools in Calgary (GA, M1356, 6, 72).

161. Stolen Generations — effects and consequences — Creative Spirits, retrieved from https://www.creativespirits.info/aboriginalculture/politics/stolen-generations/stolen- generations-effects-and-consequences

162. Zoe Laidlaw and Alan Lester Eds, Indigenous Communities and Settler Colonialism, Palgrave, 2015.

163. For more on Stretch, see Lester, Imperial Networks.

164. In 1825, Gurney published On Means of Assistance in Cases of Shipwreck and she edited The Fisherman's Friendly Visitor and Mariner's Companion. In 1830 she persuaded Trinity House to have a lighthouse installed off Happisburgh, still called the Gurney Light.

165. H. Brookman, 'Gurney, Anna (1795–1857), Old English Scholar', Oxford Dictionary of National Biography. Retrieved 15 Jan. 2019, from http://www.oxforddnb.com/ view/10.1093/ref:odnb/9780198614128.001.0001/ odnb- 9780198614128-e-11759.

166. Zoe Laidlaw 'Aunt Anna's Report': The Buxton Women and the Aborigines Select Committee, 1835–37', The Journal of Imperial and Commonwealth History, 32, 2, 2004, 18, 31.

167. Thomas Carlyle, 'Discourse on the Negro Question'. This article was first published in 1849 in Fraser's Magazine, and republished in 1853 as 'Occasional Discourse on the N****r Question'. The version reprinted in America under the title 'West India Emancipation' can be found in the University of Michigan's 'Making of America' Database and at https://cruel.org/econthought/texts/carlyle/carlodnq. html; Charles Dickens, Bleak House, ed. Nicola Bradbury, Harmondsworth, 1996, orig. 1853.

168. See Thomas C. Holt, The Problem of Freedom: Race, Labor, and Politics in Jamaica and Britain, 1832-1938, Johns Hopkins University Press, 1991 and Catherine Hall, Civilising Subjects: Colony and Metropole in the English Imagination, 1830-1867, University of Chicago Press, 2002.

References

169. Alan Lester, Etienne Nel and Tony Binns, South Africa Past, Present and Future, Prentice Hall, 2000.

170. Alan Lester, Kate Boehme and Peter Mitchell, Ruling the World: Freedom, Civilisation and Liberalism in the Nineteenth Century British Empire, Cambridge University Press, 2010. My thanks to Coel Kirkby for elaborating on some of these variations via twitter.

171. See for example James L. Fisk's guide to the Californian gold fields in the Eberstadt Collection (3N176, 2, 42) and the Report of the Commission Appointed to Enquire into the Condition of the Gold Fields of Victoria (UK National Archives NA CO 309/38, where Aboriginal people had suffered a 90 per cent decline in population by the end of the gold rushes in the early 1860s.

172. In South Africa, an initial experiment in the importation of Chinese labour for the gold mines was aborted largely because an internal system of dispossessed African migration, furthered by Rhodes and others, obviated the need.

173. https://www.mcdonaldcentre.org.uk/ethics-and-empire

174. https://www.telegraph.co.uk/politics/2022/03/28/children-should-learn-benefits-empire-says-nadhim-zahawi/

175. Kwasi Kwarteng provides a good account of the British occupation of Iraq in his Ghosts of Empire: Britain's Legacies in the Modern World, Bloomsbury, 2011.

176. German Colonialism, Suppressed Memories:

A CIGH Interview with Jürgen Zimmerer, imperialglobalexeter.co.uk

177. Neil Smith, American Empire: Roosevelt's Geographer and the Prelude to Globalization, University of California Press, 2004.

178. Shohei Sato, Britain and the Formation of the Gulf States: Embers of Empire, Manchester University Press, 2016.

179. 'Only a decade after World War II, Britain detained an entire ethnic group- nearly 1.5 million Kikuyu — in a 'pipeline' of 'rehabilitative centers' in Kenya, while concentrating half a million ethnic Chinese in Malaya's 'New Villages': Aidan Forth, Barbed Wire Imperialism: Britain's Empire of Camps, 1876–1903, U. N. Carolina Press, 2017, 12.

180. Sarah Stockwell, End of Empire, in Stockwell ed The British Empire: Themes and Perspectives, Blackwell, 2008, 277.

181. David M. Anderson, Guilty Secrets: Deceit, Denial, and the Discovery of Kenya's 'Migrated Archive', History Workshop Journal, Volume 80, Issue 1, Autumn 2015, Pages 142–160, https://doi.org/10.1093/hwj/dbv02154

182. That offer of citizenship was subsequently withdrawn from many of the children of these immigrants, by the Conservative Home Office's 'hostile environment' policy, resulting in the ongoing Windrush scandal.

183. People of colour have been a part of British society since Roman times. There is a growing body

References

of excellent historical research demonstrating the continuity of a Black presence here across many generations. See for example, David Olusoga, Black and British, A Forgotten History, Picador, 2016 and Miranda Kaufman, Black Tudors: The Untold Story, One World, 2018. But the numbers were relatively small until post-war immigration

184. Yohann Koshy, 'The Last Humanist: How Paul Gilroy Became the Most Vital Guide to our Age of Crisis', The Guardian, 5 Aug 2021.

185. Ian Sanjay Patel, We're Here Because You Were There: Immigration and the End of Empire, Verso, 2021.

186. See Amelia Gentleman, The Windrush Betrayal: Exposing the Hostile Environment, Guardian-Faber, 2020.

187. https://www.theguardian.com/books/2017/jun/03/hilary-mantel-why-i-became-a-historical-novelist#:~:text=Evidence%20is%20always%20partial.,what's%20left%20on%20the%20record.

188. Roy, The Economic History of India, 1857-1947.

189. Sunil Amrith, 'Political Culture of Health in India: a Historical Perspective', Economic and Political Weekly, 2007: https://ruralindiaonline.org/en/library/resource/political-culture-of-health-in-india-a-historical-perspective/

190. https://ourworldindata.org/health-meta

191. Quoted in Lester et al, Ruling the World, 281-2.

192. Peter Mitchell, Imperial nostalgia: How the British conquered themselves, Manchester University Press, 2021; Hannah Rose Woods,

Selective Further Reading

Rule, Nostalgia: A Backwards History of Britain, Penguin, 2022.

193. https://maxsiollun.wordpress.com/2021/06/14/nigerias-nostalgia-for-the-british-empire/

194. David Lowenthal, The Past is a Foreign Country, Cambridge University Press, 1985.

195. For a personal journey through ancestors' involvement in the slave trade and how to deal with it, see Alex Renton, Blood Legacy: Reckoning with a Family Story of Slavery, Cannongate, 2021.

196. Boris Johnson https://www.theguardian.com/ politics/2021/jun/09/notable-volleys-fired-by-ministers-in-the-culture-war

197. David Olusoga on Anita Anand and William Dalrymple, Empire podcast, episode 6: Queen Elizabeth II and Empire, Sept. 2022.

198. My thanks for Joe Kendall for sharing with me his forthcoming article 'Competitive Innocence and Defensive Memory Among Perpetrator Groups'.

199. Tory MP Says Party Must Change Attitude Towards Taking the Knee, BBC News website, 13/07/2021

200. See Joseph M. Hodge, Gerald Hödle and Martina Kopf (eds) Developing Africa: Concepts and Practices in Twentieth-Century Colonialism, Manchester University Press, 2014.

201. A. R. Dilley, 'The Economics of Empire', in Stockwell, The British Empire, 111.

202. Within the Manchester University Press Studies

References

in Imperialism series alone, see for example, Pratik Chakrabarti, Materials and medicine: Trade, conquest and therapeutics in the eighteenth century, 2014; David Hardiman, Missionaries and their medicine: A Christian modernity for tribal India, 2014; Andrew Cunningham and Bridie Andrews, Western medicine as contested knowledge, 2021; David Arnold, Imperial medicine and indigenous societies, 2021; Sabine Clarke, Science at the end of empire: Experts and the development of the British Caribbean, 1940–62, 2018; Markku Hokkanen, Medicine, mobility and the empire: Nyasaland networks, 1859–1960, 2017; Saurabh Mishra, Beastly encounters of the Raj: Livelihoods, livestock and veterinary health in North India, 1790–1920, 2015; Anna Greenwood, Beyond the state: The colonial medical service in British Africa, 2015, and Saul Dubow (ed) Science and society in southern Africa, 2009.

203. https://www.newyorker.com/news/annals-of-inquiry/how-a-conservative-activist-invented-the-conflict-over-critical-race-theory, and https://theconversation.com/amp/critical-race-theory-what-it-is-and-what-it-isnt-162752

204. War on wokeness: the year the right rallied around a made-up menace: https://www.theguardian.com/us-news/2022/dec/20/anti-woke-race-america-history?CMP=Share_iOSApp_Other

Index

abolition (of slavery) 29, 64, 98, 110, 121, 169, 178
Aden 'Emergency' 187
Afghanistan 51, 142, 144–145, 176, 201,
Amritsar Massacre 174, 176
apartheid 69, 78, 196,
Arthur, George 166
Asante 61–62, 77–78, 176

Bacon, Gareth (MP) 85, 89, 128
Bartle Frere, Sir Henry 64, 66–67, 69, 72, 76, 99, 161
Bengal 39–41, 45, 50–51, 55, 186,
Biggar, Nigel 74–75, 99, 116–118, 120, 122, 127, 174–176, 178, 180–181, 185
Black Lives Matter 13, 16, 19, 24, 29–30, 74–75, 82–83, 85, 92–94, 97, 100, 104–106, 112, 118, 128, 173, 207–208
Blyton, Enid 113–114
Brexit 19–23,
Bristol 16, 27, 30, 33, 175, 189
British South Africa Company 71–72
Buxton, Thomas Fowell 65, 154, 164–169

Canada 60–61, 133–134, 139–142, 157, 171
Carnarvon, Lord 60, 66
Carlyle, Thomas 169–171

Index

caste 54
Cawnpore 54
Chatterjee, Partha 16
Chelmsford, Lord 66
Churchill, Winston 15, 127, 184
Clayton, Sir Robert 34
Clive, Robert (statue) 32
Clive, Robert 38–42
Colston, Edward (statue) 19–23, 36, 83 96, 175
'Common Sense' (group of MPs) 79, 82, 84–86, 90–94, 127–128
Commission on Race and Ethnic Disparities (Race Report) 31, 97, 181,
Commonwealth 97–98, 100
compensation (for loss of enslaved 'property') 136
confederation 60–66
Covid 83,
Cox, Jo, MP 114–115
Culture War 115, 123, 128
Curzon, Lord 42
Cyprus insurgency 187

Dalhousie, Lord 47–51, 54, 64, 148
decolonisation 94, 100, 188, 197, 201
Delhi Durbar 148
Dickens, Charles 169–171
Dilke, Charles 60–61, 70, 74
Disraeli, Benjamin 35
Dowden, Oliver 24, 77, 79, 112

East India Company 38, 42, 45, 49, 55, 64, 90, 98, 124, 126, 134, 141, 146, 151
El Teb (Battle of) 70
English Heritage 113–114
European Union 85
Express newspaper 24, 107

famine 135–136, 148, 150–151, 169, 180
Floyd, George 19, 23, 29, 111, 122
Foreign Office 65, 119, 141, 144, 188
Fowler, Corinne 127–128,
free trade 12, 14, 89, 169, 178, 180

Gandhi, 'Mahatma' (statue) 34
GB News 24,
genocide 114, 155–156, 168, 174, 179
Gold Coast 61,
Gopal, Priyamvada 127,
Gordon, Charles 60, 70,
Great Trek 136
Guardian newspaper 29, 104,
Gurney, Anna 164–165, 167–169

Hartman, Andrew 26
Hastings, Warren 4`
Hayes, Sir John 79, 82–83, 95, 111
History Reclaimed 108, 116, 118–128, 173–174, 192, 205, 208

Hong Kong 56, 198–200
Hunter, James Davison 11, 26, 28

indentured labour 68, 90, 143, 146, 172
Independent newspaper 104,
Indian Uprising ('Mutiny') 45, 60, 77
Isandlwana (Battle of) 66, 176

Japan 145, 149
Jenrick, Robert 24, 77
Johnson, Boris 83, 96–97, 106, 115, 202

Kew Gardens 114
Kipling, Rudyard 154,
Kofi Karikari 61–62
Koh-i-Noor diamond 49

'Levelling up' (slogan) 84

Macaulay, Thomas Babington 42–43, 98–99, 150
Mail newspaper 24, 104, 107, 113–116, 127
Malaya 'Emergency' 186–187
Mandela Nelson (statue) 34
Mau Mau 'Emergency' 187–188
Mirza, Munira 31, 84, 96, 102, 104
Moore, Charles (former Telegraph editor) 106, 108, 110–112
Mughal (empire) 38, 40, 55, 149, 200

Myall Creek massacre 142–143

National Curriculum 34, 131
National Trust 41, 106–112, 116–117, 126–127
Ndebele 71–72

Olusoga, David 88, 127, 204,
Opium Wars 55–56, 145

Palmerston, Lord 56, 58–60, 132
Patel, Priti 66, 206
Powell, Enoch 188–189
Protectors of Aborigines 141
Punjab 49, 186

Railways (Indian) 147, 178
Raj 43, 147–148, 151, 172, 179, 186, 188
Randlords 72
Red River Rebellion 44, 60–61, 78
Red Wall (constituencies) 83–85, 92, 112
Residential Schools (Canada) 156–157, 179
Rhodes, Cecil 64, 69–76
Rorke's Drift (Battle of) 88, 176,
Royal African Company 21–22, 29, 34
Restore Trust lobby group 106–113, 116–117, 128, 173
Runnymede Trust 101
Russia 141, 144

Sanghera, Sathnam, 101, 127
Seacole, Mary 33–34
Sewell, Tony 96, 101
Sheffield Park 109–111
Simla Declaration 144,
Singh, Ranjit 49, 144
Singh, Duleep 49
Siraj ud-Daula 39
Slavery 15, 30, 37, 64–65, 98–99, 110, 119, 121, 126, 132, 139, 145
Spectator magazine 24, 107, 122
Stafford, Alexander (MP) 83–85
Stretch, Charles Lennox 162–163, 168
'Stolen Generation' (Australia) 159, 167
Suez 182, 186–188
Sun newspaper 104

Taiping Rebellion 58
Tasmania 166–167, 174
Telegraph newspaper 24, 104, 106–107, 109, 111, 11, 115, 122, 128
Tel el Kebir (Battle of) 70
Tombs, Robert 79
Trump, Donald 11, 27–30, 37,115, 208

Urabi Pasha 69–70

Victoria, Queen 132, 134, 148, 157

Wakefield, Edward Gibbon 140
Wilberforce, William 154

'Woke' 11,16, 24, 28, 58, 79, 84–85, 92, 94, 112–115, 122, 189
Wolseley, General (statue) 46
Wolseley, General 44–45, 54–55, 61–62, 64, 66, 69–70, 72
World War II 109, 150, 153,

Xhosa 62, 120–121, 148, 149, 158, 185–186, 193,

Zanzibar 65
Zulu 66–68

www.ingramcontent.com/pod-product-compliance
Lightning Source LLC
Chambersburg PA
CBHW061429040426
42450CB00007B/957